WHITE STAR PUBLISHERS

CONTENTS

1 In this view, the uniqueness of the chimneys on the spectacular roof of Guell Palace, designed by the architect and artist Antoni Gaudi between 1886 and 1888, can be appreciated.

2-7 This seventeenth-century print portrays an already flourishing city full of monuments, with a big and modern harbor, attesting to its strategic role in the Mediterranean.

3-6 The golden light of sunset hits behind Barcelona's port and the lively seashore drive, seen from one of the numerous terraces that look onto Montjuic.

PLACES AND HISTORY
barcelona ❧

Text and photographs by Fabrizio Finetti

Graphic design
Maria Cucchi

© 2006 White Star S.p.A.
Via Candido Sassone, 22/24
13100 Vercelli, Italy
www.whitestar.it

TRANSLATION:
AMY CHRISTINE EZRIN

ISBN: 978-88-544-0137-2

REPRINTS :
2 3 4 5 6   12 11 10 09 08

Printed in Indonesia
Color separation:
Chiaroscuro, Turin

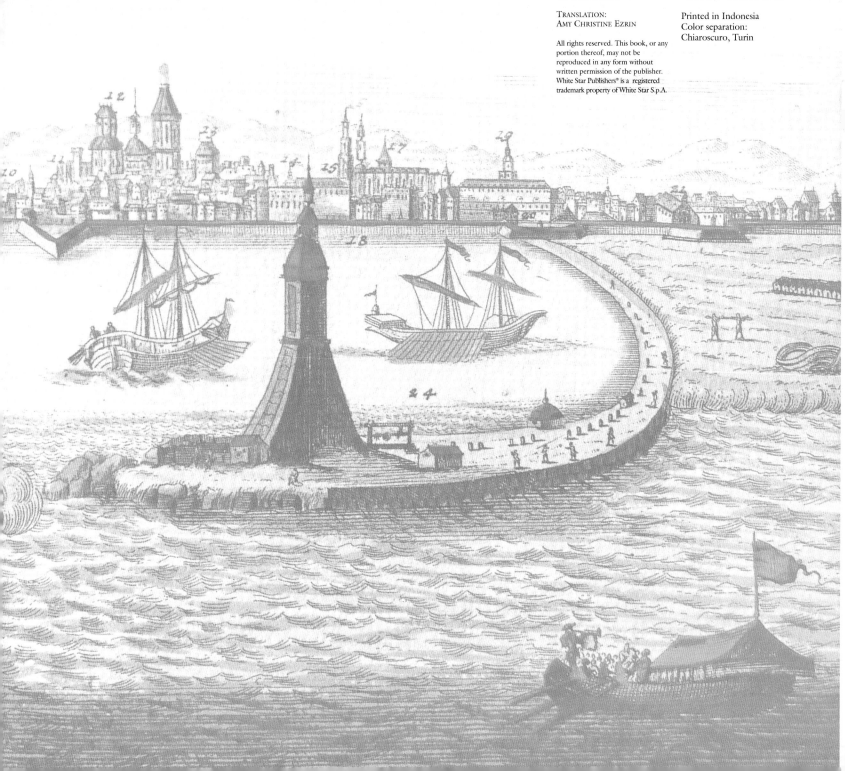

8-9 The impressive profile of the Sagrada Familia is uncontested in its domination of the Eixample Quarter, or the nineteenth-century enlargement of Barcelona, begun according to designs by urban planner Ildefons Cerdà.

A big city in Spain or the Catalan capital? This is the dilemma that Barcelona has found itself in for a thousand years, in search of both its identity and the key to deciphering its charm originating in the distant past, when traveling was for the privileged few. Perhaps more than ever before in its history, in the last twenty years the city has been facing a colossal challenge, ambitious intentions that, along with the restoration of monuments and urban planning, involve even the most essential parts of its social mosaic. Barcelona has decided to seduce the world, and like every true lover, has put in place a complex strategy to achieve its goal. Aware of its noble origins, it proudly flaunts every past honor, beginning with that attributed to it by the great Cervantes, who took refuge there after fleeing Madrid and a terrible sentence, explicitly mentioning the city in the classic *Don Quixote*, "flower among the beautiful cities of the world, the honor of Spain, the fear and dread of both declaréd and hidden enemies, the gift and delight of its inhabitants, a refuge for foreigners, ...an example of loyalty and fulfillment of all that a great, famous, rich, and well-established city could ask of a discreet and curious wish." Other cultured travelers have confirmed this shining portrait over the following centuries, such as the Englishman Henry Swinburne, who, at the end of the eighteenth century described it by saying "a side of its city walls crosses the Rambla, a wide but irregular street that they have begun to level and enlarge, with the intention of making it a central avenue.... The route is full of attractions, with peaceful lawns on one side and a series of gardens and orange groves on the other...."

Barcelona owes its splendor as a capital to enormous and tireless work, to wealth accumulated over the centuries through countless sea voyages, born of the eternal quest to achieve the dream of hegemony. Barcelona has a tenacious, hard-working, often frenetic, and at times aloof character: the Catalan nature, closed and dominating.

It has nothing in common with Andalusian Spain, sunny and sensual. Barcelona is a bourgeois Mediterranean capital, whose power was threatened and envied by the greedy Castilian nobility: irreconcilable opposites in lifestyle and mindset.

Its almost obsessive dynamism and liveliness are striking, imposing on the city a continuous self-challenge, for which reason it is as difficult to define it as it is to predict its future.

9 top left This pavilion is part of the Guell Estate, in the Pedralbes neighborhood, designed by Gaudi between 1884 and 1887, currently the location of archives and a library dedicated to Gaudi.

9 top right The central spire rises above the cathedral, erected between the end of the nineteenth century and the early years of the 1900s, an era in which the façade of the church was also completed.

10-11 Gaudi worked on the design for Guell Park from 1900 to 1914, taking his inspiration from the English concept of a garden-city. The whole park was declared part of the UNESCO World Heritage of Humanity in 1984.

10 top Three smokestacks herald the old central electric station, one of the symbols of post-industrial Barcelona, and project their shadow on the avenue of Parallel, at the base of Montjuic.

Its image can change rapidly, devouring culture and working stone and men with the same uncertain ease among business ventures, avant-gardes and poetry in the Gothic and Modernist meters. However, an archive of memories resists this regenerative earthquake, preserving a black and white portrait unknown to tourists: photographs in which traces remain of its industrial and anarchist soul with the remnants of poor areas and crumbled walls.

With these non-places "where the city loses its name," Barcelona could be any post-industrial metropolis, which however passionately cultivates the memory of timeless geniuses and lets itself be caressed by the Mediterranean breeze.

The Mediterranean is the point: it is worth remembering the words and sensations of those who have fully experienced living in this city, even in recent times, to understand how this common denominator surfaces so forcefully.

For Manuel Vazquez Montalban, its favorite son, Barcelona "remains a port city at heart" and therefore "a city of passage, at whose door the fragments of all that travels accumulate."

At this threshold, the port, Gabriele Basilico noticed "the sound and presence of iron," as he remembers that "closing my eyes, the odors of the world can be smelled."

10

11 top The ancient factory of Casaramona, the work of Josep Puig I Cadafalch (1911), is one of the most beautiful examples of industrial architecture from the Modernist period.

Just like Cervantes, George Moustaki found in Barcelona a safe harbor, "a fraternal homeland, born of the same Mediterranean mother."

Then, there is the memory of George Orwell, who recalled: "I used to sit on the roof marveling at the craziness of all of it... one sight after the other of tall and slender buildings, glass domes and fanciful, curvaceous roofs in bright green and copper-colored tiles. Further to the east, the sparkling clear blue sea: the first view of the sea that I have had since my arrival in Spain."

Even more fitting to the present-day reality and the city's desire to attract the attention of the world are the words of Pablo Picasso, a man that enjoyed the existence of Barcelona as much as possible. They include those words thought while "drawing the color of its memory, its rainbow voice." This unabashed declaration of love for Barcelona was stated by the artist in a language charged with futurist sensuality.

It is an explicit invitation to those who wish to be unconditionally overwhelmed by the rhythm of life, "from the smell of fish and watermelon and pure cigar smoke and clams and basil, to later on at two-thirty or three in the morning on the Barceloneta beach on the Eve of Saint John, swathed in a sheet of silk...."

14-15 In this panoramic photograph, the city is seen from the mountain of Tibidabo. In the foreground, the neighborhoods born of the long industrial boom of the 1960s can be seen, and in the background, with the unmistakable profile of the Olympic towers, Barcelona overlooking the sea.

IBERIAN ROOTS TO A MEDITERRANEAN DREAM

16 A thirteenth-century miniature portraying a battle between Christians and Muslims. Barcelona found itself to be the frontier between the Arab and Christian worlds several times, but although it lived almost the entire eighth century under Muslim domination, it has not preserved any significant traces from this period.

B arcelona's deepest roots cling to the rocky slopes of Montjuic like they do the fertile Catalan fields, inhabited since the Paleolithic era, right up until the origin of the Iberian civilization. Nevertheless, it was the Romans who gave a definite face to the settlement, living side by side with the natives since the third century B.C., during their unstoppable conquest of the peninsula. Once the wars with Carthage ended and the *pax romana* was established, the village on the Montjuic soon grew insufficient and people began to populate the surrounding plains. The colony of Barcino, from the endless name of Colonia Iulia Augusta Faventia Paterna Barcino, was settled at the end of the first century B.C. (between 15 and 10 B.C.), at the time of Augustus, on a slight rise on the plains called the Mons Taber.

It was a successful choice, as the city soon discovered its vocation for maritime commerce and flourished in the shadow of the powerful Tarraco (Tarragona) colony, while it also played an important role in trade along the Augustan Way thanks to the territory's agricultural and mining activities.

In the imperial era, Barcino was a small city but had an intense public life, which already suffered for lack of open spaces, even though in the fifth century it preferred not to enlarge its perimeter but to reinforce the already existing one by building 74 towers. Once the empire of the West collapsed, a long period of instability began in which the Iberian Peninsula was the setting for disputes between the Visigoths and Ostrogoths.

These centuries have furnished the earliest evidence of the existence of a Christian community to which the legendary figure of Saint Eulalia belonged. This period was marked by the great shadow of the Dark Ages and important-sounding names, like Ataulfo, the successor of Alarico, who converted the city into the capital of his kingdom in 415 with his bride Galla Placidia. This was but an insignificant aside in history since, in 416, Ataulfo lost his life and with him went the dream of peace. In 531, the Visigoths again named Barcelona the capital, but it was another fleeting illusion, extinguished in the transfer of the court to Toledo. The Muslim Conquest followed in 717, taking place in a particularly gentle way and lasting for the whole eighth century, without leaving any significant monuments or modifications to the city structure.

17 Legend has it that the young Eulalia, thereafter proclaimed a saint and the city's patron, went to the Roman governor Dacian at the time of Diocletian to protest the persecution of Christians. For the insolence demonstrated, the girl was imprisoned and condemned to suffer a number of tortures equal to that of her age.

However, Barcelona became the frontier between the Islamic world and the Carolingian Empire, to which they literally opened their gates in 801, welcoming the troops of Ludovic the Pious. This gesture was rewarded by the Franks by liberating the city of the vassalage typical of the feudal world and giving them ample economic freedom. As a bastion at the edges of the empire, Barcelona became the seat of a count-governor favored by the Carolingian monarchy. At the end of the ninth century, Wilfred the Hairy, the count of Urgell, took into his hands the counties of Gerona, Barcelona and Osona and laid the basis for hereditary rule. The event marked the start of a gradual distancing from Frankish dominion, completed under the mandate of Borrell II (947-992), during which time the re-

gion became formally independent and began its political and commercial rise over the following centuries. Independence ensured the city the role of being a natural meeting point for Western and Arab cultures but was unable to save it from devastating incursions and sackings, like that of 985, which reduced it to ashes. Once these terrible waves were overcome, the medieval city had by now come into existence, skilled at acquiring political autonomy as a true cushion state, while the Catalan state slowly took form. The privileges conceded by the Franks, the city's transformation into an independent county and the strategic role played by commerce have

been mentioned, but there is no doubt that it was Barcelona's alliance with the Aragonese Crown that elevated it, in the twelfth century, to being the capital of a small Mediterranean empire. Precisely in that century, the traits of the national identity formed, from the apparition of the name Cataluna to the written use of the Catalan language. It was the genesis of the dream that moved the city, born on solid rock, to seek its fortune at sea, to the east. The steps of this expansion coincided with the Christian conquest of the peninsula, which happened throughout the twelfth and thirteenth centuries across a wide area between the mouth of the

Ebro River and Valencia to the south and beyond the Pyrenees to the north. In those years, the marriage of Berenger IV and Petronilla, the heir to the throne of Aragon (1137), marked the height of the power of the counts and the birth of a confederation of independent kingdoms united under the name of the Aragonese Crown. With Alfonso I and Peter I the Catholic, the new state was firmly united and ready to expand its borders. With James I those confines surpassed the limits of the mainland for the first time; during his reign, which lasted for an extraordinary 63 years, the Baleari Islands were occupied between 1229 and 1235.

18-19 Pere Martell proposes the conquest of Majorca to King Jaume I during a banquet held in Tarragona, from the Chronicles of Jaume I *in the historical archives of Barcelona.*

19 Berenguer IV, portrayed by Filippo Ariosto in this sixteenth century tablet conserved in the military museum, left a profound mark on Barcelona's history.

As its realm grew, the city expanded beyond its old walls, creating new neighborhoods clustered around churches and monasteries that for the entire Middle Ages would hold the irreplaceable function of meeting places, besides that of being the main source for spreading culture throughout the region. The need to protect these new boroughs brought about the construction of a second wall enclosure that started in 1260 and whose perimeter was over three miles long: the first true major urban development in its history. With goods being traded men arrived speaking every known language, since the city's merchants were landing on all the shores of the Mediterranean, including those of faraway Egypt. Such a complex socio-economic situation necessitated an equally effective law, which was passed between the twelfth and the thirteenth century. It was a collection of normatives and procedures that originated in Roman and Visigoth law later enriched with privileges and immunities conceded under Frankish rule. The *usatges*, which could be essentially translated as "uses" or "customs," became the legal basis for everything, a true civil and commercial code on which medieval Catalan society was based.

Contemporaneously, a political evolution followed that saw the power of the counts and, thereafter, the royalty expand to a wider base, such as during the thirteenth century when the highest Catalan institutions were founded, the *Cortes e la Generalitat*. Whereas previously the functions of civil government were performed only by the figure of the *veguer*, an official of the king, in 1258, under James I, eight councilmen and an assembly of 200 judges, reduced to 100 in 1265, were added to the cabinet of the members of government (the four *veguers*). This *Consell de Cent*, or the earliest Catalan parliamentary institution, was abolished only in 1714.

A contribution from an influential Jewish component could not be lacking in a society with such developed economic relations, and this community was documented as present since the mid-ninth century. In Catalonia, the *aljamas*, as Jewish communities on Spanish Christian lands were called, lived under the direct protection of the crown in neighborhoods known as *calls*, reserved especially for their economic and religious activities, whereas the function of chancellor was held by the *battle*, a figure that had the duty of directly administering even the royal assets.

20 top A manuscript portraying the family celebration of a Jewish holiday. The first evidence documenting a Jewish presence in Catalonia dates back to the mid-ninth century and refers precisely to the city of Barcelona.

20 bottom The Usatges de Barcelona, *found in a fourteenth-century manuscript, were the first collection of legal normatives from* different origins. *Assembled starting in the twelfth century, they served to regulate various aspects of civil and commercial life at the time.*

21 *This fifteenth-century engraving shows the port of Barcelona after the completion of construction on an artificial wharf.*

The policy of the Aragonese Crown, favored by strong social cohesion and great entrepreneurial capacities, led Barcelona towards the era of its highest splendor, characterized by predominantly commercial expansion more than by secure territory conquests.

The steps of this movement towards the east saw the city first confront their rivalry with Genoa and then with Venice for maritime supremacy, while conquests and annexations obligated it to set up consulates and armed fleets to protect their ships along the main Mediterranean routes. James I's reign was followed by that of Peter II the Great (1276-1285), who occupied Sicily in 1285, and then that of James II the Just (1291-1327), during which, in 1303, Roger de Flor pushed as far as Constantinople with an expedition called the La Gran Compania Catalana, or the Catalan Company.

The campaign lasted until 1311 and, apart from defeating the Turks, ended in the occupation of even the Duchies of Athens and Neopatria. During James II's reign, Sardinia was also conquered, between 1323 and 1324, thus achieving total hegemony on the western Mediterranean shores.

The result of the conquests could be none other than a glow of magnificence and wealth, which bore the splendor of French Gothic.

This style may have worked its way beyond the powerful walls of Romanesque Catalan later than in other places, but it left behind the greatest of examples with splendid churches like those in both private residences and the palaces of the ruling class.

Some workshops received new inspiration whereas other started from scratch. The cathedral, the churches of St. Maria del Mar and St. Maria del Pi, the Pedralbes Monastery, the Llotja, the Ospedale of the Holy Cross and the palaces of Carrer Montcada are only a few examples of this extraordinary period that saw Barcelona change its image and size by incorporating the Raval quarter and finishing its impressive defensive system.

Construction of the third wall enclosure, begun by Peter III around the mid-1300s, completed the previous defensive structure, reinforcing the side along the sea and, as mentioned before, enlarging the city to the west in the direction of Montjuic.

Of the entire perimeter, today only the portal of Santa Madrona, near the sea, has been preserved, but the layout of the city at that time remains an indelible mark on its physiognomy, as it still outlines the neighborhoods of the old city, broken only by the nineteenth-century expansion of the *eixample*.

However, the greatest paradox of the era is undoubtedly represented by the lack of a port – an incredible fact, to say the least, for an economy sus-

tained by maritime trade. Once the old landing point at the base of the Montjuic was abandoned, the city only had a beach naturally protected by a few little islands at its disposition. Impossible to dock any medium- to large-sized ships, it was necessary to unload goods with a continuous back-and-forth of small boats, an activity that employed a large number of men, from boaters to porters.

24 top left Alfonso IV of Catalonia and Alfonso V of Aragon, known as "the magnanimous," were painted in a portrait by Filippo Ariosto (sixteenth century). Author of an expansionist policy, after the conquest of Naples in 1443, the king also decided to transfer his court there, thus causing the further decline of Barcelonese hegemony.

Paradox for paradox, construction of an artificial port began only in the fifteenth century, by now at the twilight of Catalan maritime power.

The height of the city's splendor and its decline crossed paths as early as the first half of the 1300s, during the reign of Peter III.

There is no doubt that one of the main causes of its decline was the dramatic demographic crisis set off by continual epidemics, culminating in the infamous black plague of 1348 that hit all of Europe, not sparing Catalonia, and during which almost all the members of the Consell de Cent died.

The difficult situation during those years, nonetheless, did not interrupt maritime trade, actually favoring speculative phenomena and a consequential concentration of capital.

These circumstances allowed for the wealth of a part of the mercantile class to grow but exasperated social tensions as the large majority of the population was decimated by hunger and famine.

Though the city's inhabitants were reduced to only 20,000 by 1392, the splendid palace of the Llotja was inaugurated, and in 1401, the Taula de Canvi of Barcelona, or the first European exchange, was opened, where the most important currencies of the era circulated.

The death of King Martin the Humane, in 1410, marked the end of the Catalan-Aragonese Crown and set off a fight over the succession. The passage of power to the Castilian Trastamara dynasty initiated a tragic period in the city's existence, marked in particular by the expansionist policy of Alfonso the Magnanimous who, having conquered Naples in 1443, transferred his court there after a short time.

Barcelona suddenly found itself losing its hegemonic position, while the internal conflict between the royal power and the people, voiced by the Generalitat, was also sharpening. Two citizen faction groups were the main characters in this clash, the Biga and the Busca, culminating in the dramatic civil war of 1462 and ending with the peace treaty of Pedralbes of 1472. During the reign of Fernando II, at the end of the century, the Catalan population reached its lowest levels in history, around 250,000 individuals, as great geographical discoveries shifted world trade routes to the Atlantic.

To such a ravaged social and economic situation was added the persecution of Jews, fed by the ambitions of the monarchy as well as the intransigence of the clergy. The pillaging and murder had already begun by the end of the fourteenth century, to the extent that in 1401, Martin the Humane declared the *aljamas* of Barcelona eliminated. However, with the final expulsion of the rich Jewish community by the realms of Aragon and Castile (1492), the city took a further step towards total decline.

26 bottom The engraving Barcelona in Spain *by Daniel Meisner illustrates the city as it appeared between 1627 and 1631.*

26-27 The port and city of Barcelona are outlined well in this engraving held in the city's museum of history. Worth noting, the area on which the

Barceloneta neighborhood would be built in the mid-1700s appears to the right of the wharf.

27 top This view of Barcelona taken from Civitates Orbis Terrarum *by G. Braun shows the Catalan city in 1576, already a flourishing Mediterranean port.*

At the beginning of the 1500s, Barcelona and Catalonia were only the peripheral provinces of a vast empire that stretched from Asia to the Americas, once again a borderland between France and the Turkish power that infested the seas. Resisting the authoritarian and centralist pressures of the crown, the city managed to maintain its autonomy though without having any way to intervene in general affairs. In this shifting era, Barcelona built its fame for being a hard-working city and confirmed its first great vocation: trade. Traits of this strong and volatile character can be sought in the *gremios,* the ancient corporations that had slowly formed a compact and active social fabric. Originating in the thirteenth century from out of the ancient religious fraternities, the corporations soon abandoned their role as aid-providers to handle the defense of economic interests through control of prices and the market. When the golden era of the sea trade ended, Barcelona was able to cultivate a new source of wealth within its walls, producing textiles, glassware, leather, metal, and even more importantly, it managed to have representatives from this powerful artisan community be seated in the city's political institutions.

For the sake of continuity, the *gremios* maintained a central role in civil life, until the new system of production imported from the industrial revolution was established. The general decline of the sixteenth century seriously hindered the spread of the Renaissance in Catalonia and allowed for a period of only modest artistic development, although it is worth remembering that it was during those years that the Ramblas, considered until then a simple border line between the city and the Raval, took on a centrality and importance thanks to the new religious structures inspired by the Counter-Reformation.

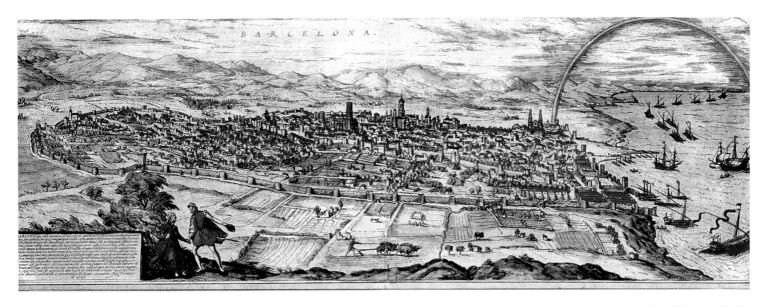

BARCINO. BARCELONA.

13. La Gallerie près
14. Le Barreau
15. S. Marie de la Mer
16. S. Cathrine
17. La Douanne
18. La Place d'Armes
19. La Place ou Pont d'M.
20. Nost. Dame d'Mont.
21. Le Fanal du Molle
24. Tours de Merides
26. Montserrat
27. Le Port:

Political crisis and religious fanaticism interacted for decades in a climate of authentic persecution, made legendary by the terrible Spanish Inquisition, while growing economic marginalization continued to further exasperate the clash between the ruling Catalan class and the Spanish monarchy.

As a result, with Philip IV ruling, the day of Corpus Domini came in 1640, when the Dels Segadors (The Harvesters) revolt exploded – a popular rebellion incited by the presence of the Castilian troops on Catalan land.

The fight soon transformed into a political revolution that saw the Generalitat ally with France to take back their lost independence, but in 1652, after the collapse of alliances and a long siege, Barcelona accepted the imperial conditions: general amnesty and the preservation of formal autonomy. Far from the Gothic splendors and Renaissance esthetics, a dogmatic, overstated and pessimistic form of baroque became widespread. The worst was yet to come.

The death of Charles II, in 1700, unleashed a long battle over his succession among the European powers, which saw the Aragonese Crown support the archduke Charles of Austria (Charles III) against the designated heir, Philip V.

The clash culminated in a harsh siege withstood by the Barcelonese for over a year, finally ending tragically on September 11, 1714. The conclusion marked the end of their freedom and the centuries-old Catalan institutions.

Once the repression relented, however, the city's impressive survival instinct surfaced, its population quadrupling by the end of the century and the foundations were rapidly laid for the industrial revolution. Specialization of agricultural production and the renovation and vast development of the textile industry (cotton especially) made it possible for Barcelona to appear again on the great commercial routes now directed towards America.

The Bourbon city resumed a dynamic pace, expanding along the sea with the big urban-development project of the Barceloneta (1735), whereas the Ramblas had by now become its spinal column.

Even cultural and scientific development during the second half of the eighteenth century was tied to economic enterprises because they were given incentive from private institutions, like the various academies and the board of trade, which were feeling the effects of government repression less.

Planta de la Ciutat de Barcelona, Fortalesas, y Atacos.

30 The engraving, held in the National Library of Madrid, portrays the taking of the citadel and the castle of Montjuic by French troops on February 29, 1808.

30-31 The Arch of Triumph, portrayed here in a late-nineteenth-century photo, was built on the occasion of the 1888 World Expo, an event that deeply marked the shape of the city.

31 bottom left The inauguration of the monument to Columbus on June 1, 1888, coincided with the celebration of the first world exposition hosted by Barcelona.

31 bottom right In this 1873 engraving, the popular celebrations held in Plaça St. Jaume for the proclamation of the First Republic are recorded.

The end of the eighteenth century heralded a century of wars and revolutions that began with the fight against Napoleonic expansionism (the so-called *guerra contra el frances*, or "war against the Frenchman") from 1808 to 1814 and concluded in internal tensions in response to the tough restoration of Fernando VII.

History was accelerating and the dates began to overlap in a series of popular triumphs and frustrated rebellions. The third and fourth decades of the nineteenth century saw struggles between the liberal, moderate and progressive factions against the absolute monarchy, but records also report dramatic episodes like the fire of the convents in 1835 and the two bombings of the city in 1842-43.

Pragmatic Barcelona, heedless of the ways of the soul, experimented with steam power and its application to railroads and shipping to transform industry and transportation methods and inaugurated the first Spanish metalworks in the mid-1800s. The industrial revolution and overturning of consciences marched on side by side with the rise of the workers' movement. The city was

exploding. Old Barcelona was desperately searching for space, opened up by knocking down convents and palaces to make way for markets and lodging for the commoners, a prelude to the destruction of the walls that began in 1854. The limits of the medieval city were surpassed; Barcelona intended to rationally expand without end according to the futuristic plan of the *eixample* (the enlargement) by Idlefons Cerdà. A social utopia more than an urban revolution, the *manzanas*, or the blocks, were supposed to be built up on only two sides, leaving all the rest to gardens, parks and public places. It was about ennobling the new and wealthy bourgeoisie, now that they were finally free to shape their own space and identity. Of course, politics and private interests could only mutilate the grandiose design, emptying it of all ideological substance and preserving only its urban value, all while wars and governments did not allow space for social peace and quiet.

It was the era of the revolution of September 1868, of the third *carlista* war, of the first republic (1873) and of the immediate Bourbon restoration,

which ensured a brief period of political stability through the figure of Alfonso XII, the so-called "gold fever" for the Barcelonese bourgeoisie. Though opposed by the Catalan political movement, the great World's Fair was opened in 1888 and set up on an area of over 4,000,000 square feet that encompassed the present-day Citadel Park, Francia Station and a tract of the Barceloneta, of which a few pieces had been preserved, among them the famous triumphal arch that was the entrance to the enclosure.

The occasion, besides outlining the entire area of the park, served to accelerate plans for urban interventions that involved the whole seaside, including the design of a monument to Christopher Columbus inaugurated on June 1, 1888.

Not to be forgotten, at the same time the other Barcelona was celebrating the foundation of the Workers' General Union, a socialism-inspired union at the heart of which an anarchical and revolutionary current developed.

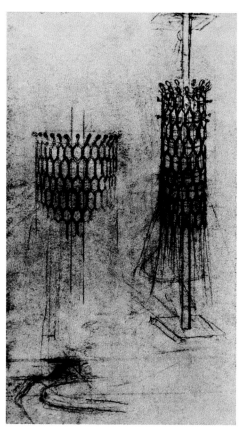

Between 1800 and 1900, the clash between two opposite instincts was being outlined: the constructive one of Modernism and the chaotic one of anarchism. The first originated in the intention to create a unique Catalan style, in sync with the strongest of nationalist sentiments and in line with the cultural beliefs started by the Renaixença (Renaissance) movement, but open to the new trends of the European avant-garde. Modernism imposed on architecture, literature and theater; but above all, it brought art to everyday life, generating furniture, enamels, stained glass and everything that could lend a noble character with a seal of originality to the new bourgeois lifestyle. These were the years of Antoni Gaudi and many other artists that left behind an indelible mark on the city's image.

33 top Gaudi shows the on-going construction of the Sagrada Familia to the apostolic delegate Monsignor Ragonesi, accompanied by the bishop of Barcelona Rey i Casanovas, on July 2, 1915.

Unfortunately, the first few decades of the twentieth century saw the confrontation between the oppressed social classes explode with a series of events that gave Barcelona the sad epithet of the city of bombs, thanks to the attacks of 1893 and 1896 and the revolt of the "Tragic Week" of 1909, which was followed by tough repression.

Thus, while on one hand the Lliga Regionalista was formed in 1901, becoming the leading party of political Catalanism, and the Mancomunitat (the first institution of self-government since 1714) was inaugurated in 1914, on the other hand, the CNT (the National Labor Confederation) was constituted in 1910, destined to become the strongest union in the Catalan workers' movement, leading the city to the general strike of 1919 and the concession of an eight-hour work day. Fear and vendettas generated a climate of authentic social war, the ideal situation for the authoritarian solution that was not long in coming.

On September 13, 1923, with the approval of Alfonso XIII, Miguel Primo de Rivera took power and, in addition to unleashing a brutal repression on the workers' movement, also wiped out the accomplishments and hopes of longed-for Catalan autonomy.

Nonetheless, the city had never slowed down its productive pace and still pursued the opportunity for international exposure that came with the second great exposition, opened in May, 1929.

EXPOSICIÓN INTERNACIONAL BARCELONA 1929

36 top left A demonstration takes place in front of the Catalonian Parliament, in 1934. The brief existence of the Second Republic, begun in 1932, ends in October of 1934, when the central government with the help of the army deposes the president of the Generalitat,

Lluis Companyis, for having proclaimed the Catalan State within the Spanish Federal Republic.

36 top right Political propaganda in the streets during the years of the Civil War (1936-39) was particularly heated and virulent. The gravely tense situation

that was created in the country during the years of the Republic soon found the spark needed to set off the conflict. The revolt broke out on July 17, 1936 in Morocco against the republican government and soon spread to the national territory, with the resultant tragic consequences.

This time, the exhibition stimulated urban development even more, involving many neighborhoods beyond that of the area at the base of Montjuic, now transformed into one big monumental complex. The fall of the dictatorship in 1930 also marked the end of the monarchy and, in the elections of the following April, the happily unanticipated triumph of the Esquerra Repubblicana, the party that had reunited the various Catalanist currents.

The second republic allowed for the approval of the new autonomous statutes in September of 1932 and, two years later, the proclamation of the Catalan State within the Spanish Federal Republic.

Barcelona briefly experienced the illusion of being a capital city, soon frustrated, however, by a coup d'état against the republic. The sparking of the internal conflict found its fuse in the military revolt of July 17, 1936: the civil war was in the streets of the whole nation. The dramatic chapter lasted a good three years, carrying with it disastrous and long-lasting consequences, increased by the downfall of democratic and republican Spain and then by the Second World War.

The victorious nationalist right, with Francisco Franco Bahamonde at its head, established a regime of ruthless retaliation in 1939, which within a few years had executed thousands of opposition members and, obviously, wiped out every possible form of political, social and cultural autonomy.

36-37 The armed battle in the streets of Barcelona during the civil war was bitter and dramatic. This photograph by Agustì Centelles, shot on July 19, 1936, documents the first day of fighting in the Catalan capital.

37 top Barcelona was also subjected to the outrage of bombs. In the photograph, the effects of aerial bombing on March 18, 1938, can be clearly seen.

37 bottom The president of the Generalitat Lluis Companyns is portrayed in this electoral poster of the "Front d'Esquerras," a coalition of leftist Catalan parties that triumphed in the February 16, 1936, elections.

38 top Madrid, July 1969: the "generalisimo" Francisco Franco proclaims Price Juan Carlos as successor to the crown before the Cortes.

38-39 On July 25, 1992, Barcelona's Olympic dream was achieved, with the glorious opening ceremony of the twenty-fifth edition of the games in the stadium of Montjuic.

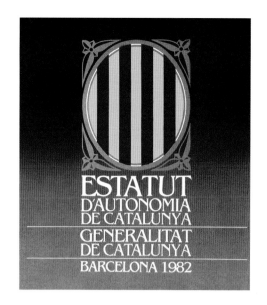

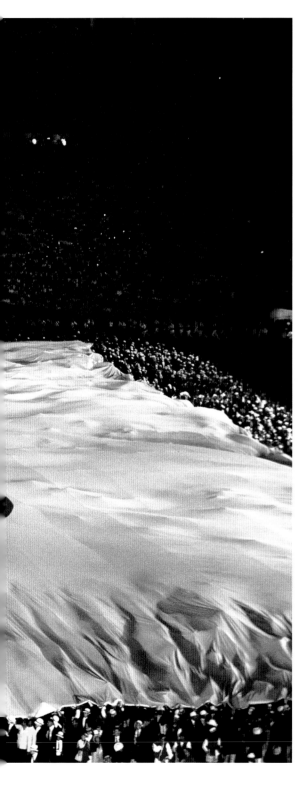

The long post-war period and Spain's autarkic isolation brought about the collapse of the Catalan economy, which only resumed movement in the 1960s through the initiation of an impressive and long cycle of development.

Two events decided the end of Francoism and the passage to democracy. In 1969, the "generalisimo" designated the present-day king Juan Carlos of Bourbon as his successor and, in 1973, an attack on Carrero Blanco (head of the executive committee) by ETA, the Basque liberation party, eliminated the true heir to the dictatorship.

Franco died on November 20, 1975, and the following year, Adolfo Suarez, appointed the first president of the government by the king, initiated a quick shift towards democracy. With the elections of June 1977 and the immense demonstration on September 11 in the same year, Catalonia once again stated its autonomist will with astounding force, burning things at stops along the procession. On September 29 the Generalitat was reactivated and in the following month Josep Tarradellas returned from exile in France and assumed command. Tarradellas then formed a government of a vast coalition that worked intensely to create the new autonomous statutes, approved on October 25, 1979. We are in the present: the text of the statutes recognizes the Generalitat as the governing institution, with the incorporation of a parliament, an executive committee and a president, a role represented by Jordi Pujol from 1980 to 2003. Finally, the city, free to manage its enormous resources, could reinstate its challenge to the whole world. The spark flew on October 17, 1986, when it was designated to host the 25th Olympic Games, celebrated with great success in 1992. It was a memorable event not only for its results but, above all, for the perfect organization. Barcelona discovered that it had a formidable engine within and an innate capacity to look ahead. In addition to the total and umpteenth urban overhaul, the Catalans were betting on showing the world a new image and jotting down the basis for the Barcelona of the future: the city of the art of knowing how to live.

*41 top left Our Lady
of Grace (la Mercé)
protects the
neighborhood bearing
its name from atop
the eighteenth-century
church dedicated to
her.*

*40 Light and shadow
ceaselessly shape the
buildings in the
Gothic Barrio, the
heart of the city and a
true labyrinth of
streets and people. In
the photograph, the
arch on Carrer del
Bisbe.*

*40-41 Though its
form was only
completed in the last
century, the
unmistakable outline
of the cathedral
represents the most
important Gothic
element in the eclectic
skyline of Barcelona.*

On the Ramblas, between the Gothic Barrio and the Raval, as far as the sea and the Barceloneta.

The ancient center of the city is an irregular hexagon facing the sea with the eighteenth-century appendix of the Barceloneta: it is the heart that attracts the world's interest, as much for its Gothic wonders as for its extravagant humanity.

A labyrinth of gray stone where centuries of history, legends, wealth and desperation are concentrated, it is increasingly becoming a commercial as well as cultural display window, though still the soul of a metropolis that never tires of living and astounding. Our intense journey begins with a leap back in time from the Plaça del Rei, in search of Roman foundations, the historical origin of Barcino. The city's Museum of History holds the machine able to overcome the 2,000 years separating us from its foundation.

In the fourteenth-century Padellas House, an underground archaeological itinerary, excavated from a 43,000 square feet area where important Roman and Visigoth artifacts were recovered over 30 years of work, departs from the institution. The excavations documented are datable to between the first and seventh centuries A.D., among which stand out a Roman-era craftsmen's area and a bishop's complex, a Visigoth-era group of buildings devoted to the Christian worship, located in a vast area behind a tract of walls. Particularly well done is the reconstruction of Visigoth-era daily life in ancient Barcino, which shows how the small colony was devoted to trade, exporting wine and garum (a fish-based sauce) throughout the empire. Besides the excavations, the museum also features two medieval gems: the magnificent Gothic hall of the Tinell, from 1370, and the chapel of St. Agata, both incorporated into the complex of the Royal Palace, the seat of the counts and the sovereigns of Barcelona. The square forms a harmonic ensemble, symbolically completed by a modern sculpture by Edoardo Chillida and dominated by the curious sixteenth-century outline of the tower of King Martin the Humane.

41 top right This room belongs to the Frederic Mares Museum, founded by the sculptor himself in 1946 and composed of his collections, among which his collection of ancient sculptures holds particular importance.

42 The cathedral is illuminated in the colors of the holiday in this lovely nighttime photograph.

43 left Construction on the cathedral began at the end of the thirteenth century, completed only in 1915.

The exit in the direction of the Carrer de la Pietat features the magnificent apse of the cathedral with its intense play of light and shadow and the entrance to the original cloister finished in 1448, surrounded on three sides by 20 chapels and home to 13 geese, the symbol of purity of St. Eulalia, the city's patron saint. The cathedral, dedicated to the same saint, is a masterpiece of imposing dimensions, built during the golden years of Catalan power, between 1298 and the end of 1400, and containing important works of art in the 28 chapels lining its perimeter.

However, dominating the scene in the middle of the nave is the majestic wooden choir, the work of Bartolomé Ordonez and Pedro Villar, with its Renaissance-style marble enclosure where, in 1519, the Order of the Golden Toson gathered for the first time. Like a treasury of the faith, the cathedral also safeguards the crucifix of Lepanto, which, according to legend, comes directly from the figurehead of the ship of Don Juan D'Austria, a veteran of the historic battle against the Turks in 1571.

Finally, in the crypt of the cathedral rests the body of the young martyr, St. Eulalia. Legend tells of the attempted mutilate of the body by religious fanatics as it was being moved into the cathedral.

Unexplainably, the procession stopped and soon after an angel appeared and pointed to the sacrilege with its finger: the saint was asking to not enter the cathedral if she were to be worshiped disfigured.

43 right A stained-glass window elegantly demonstrates the ornamental profusion on the cathedral's façade.

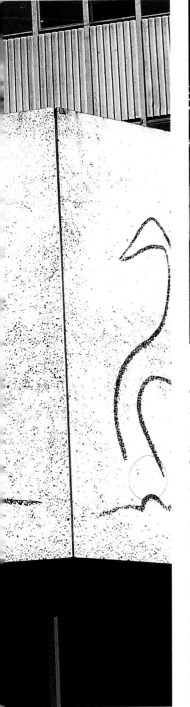

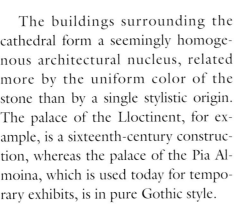

The buildings surrounding the cathedral form a seemingly homogenous architectural nucleus, related more by the uniform color of the stone than by a single stylistic origin. The palace of the Lloctinent, for example, is a sixteenth-century construction, whereas the palace of the Pia Almoina, which is used today for temporary exhibits, is in pure Gothic style.

Ca l'Ardiaca, firmly anchored to the Roman towers, is also a fourteenth-century construction that contains a small Renaissance fountain in its little courtyard, famous for holding the traditional "dancing egg" on Corpus Christi Day. The headquarters of the Marès Museum, on the other hand, belongs to the multi-sectioned complex of the Royal Palace and holds the collections donated by its founder, the sculptor Eugeni Marès.

Blocked on three sides, the cathedral finds an adequate exit only on the modeled square in front of its portal, which forms a unique combination with the *placa nova* and represents an exemplary blend of seemingly irreconcilable eras and styles.

Its late-nineteenth century façade and spires, free to express their vertical hymn, emerge from the mighty Roman walls, at whose base the modern letters of Joan Brossa can be read, forming the world Barcino, in tribute to the birth of Barcelona.

46 and 47 top right
The palace of the
Generalitat is an
institution symbolic of
the thousand years of
Catalan
independence. The
palace, apart from its
main façade on Plaça
St. Jaume, has a
gorgeous side
entrance, the work of
Marc Safont in the
fifteenth century.

46-47 Despite its
neoclassical
appearance, the town
hall in Plaça St.
Jaume safeguards a
much older nucleus,
in which the Hall of
the Consell de Cent
(the Council of the
Hundred) stands out,
an institution started
in the fourteenth
century, the
forerunner of a true
Catalan parliament.

Having enjoyed that spectacular sight, one can explore step by step the fascinating complex of buildings and lanes in the Gothic Barrio, whose name is an invention of the 1920s, as is the arch of Carrer del Bisbe, since become a symbol that seems to unite the area of religious power with that of political power.

The monumental palaces of Plaça Sant Jaume, a meeting point of the two main Roman-era roads, contain the town hall and the Generalitat – the Catalan government, an emblem of their thousand years of autonomy. The first was conceived to not only be an administrative building but also a true collection of works of art open to the public every Sunday. Despite its nineteenth-century façade, it is a Gothic building safeguarding within it the hall of the Consell de Cent (inaugurated in 1373), the historic institution of city government active since 1714.

The Generalitat, on the other hand, which started in the early fourteenth century, stands on the square with a harmonic Renaissance appearance, despite having maintained on Carrer del Bisbe a beautiful lateral façade in Catalan-Gothic style from the first half of the 1400s and an elegant staircase, both works by Marc Safont (Barcelona, fifteenth century). On April 23, St. George's ("Jordi" in Catalan) Day, both the buildings open to welcome the traditional blessing of the roses, almost a national Catalan holiday.

47 top left The neo-Gothic arch on Carrer del Bisbe makes for one of the most charming views in old Barcelona, along the obligatory route between St. Jaume Square and the cathedral.

48 *A spectacular, nine-story human castle rises in Placa St. Jaume during the festivities of the Mercé (Our Lady of Grace), which take place in September throughout the city.*

49 *The exhibitions of the Castellers are one of the most important manifestations of Catalan folklore and an indispensable ingredient in any respectable holiday celebration. Besides the forms and characteristics that these human towers can take on, they perfectly represent the spirit of solidarity and the strong cohesion that are still part of the foundations of Catalan society.*

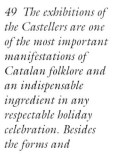

49

50 top The solemn and radiant window that runs around the interior of the auditorium in the Palau de la Music in Barcelona is decorated with floreal motifs in the shape of wreaths.

50 center The violin-playing muse, the work of Lluis Bru and Eusebi Arnau, is one of the female figures adorning the half-circle of the orchestra pit in the auditorium of the Palau de la Musica.

50 bottom Some musicians rehearse in the auditorium of the Palau de la Musica, originally the home of the Orfeo Català, a chorus founded in 1891.

50-51 The "delirious" concert hall in Palau de la Musica Catalana, a masterpiece of Lluis Domenech i Montaner, was inaugurated in 1908 and is able to accommodate 2,000 spectators.

Outside the square, the neighborhood resumes its more intimate physiognomy composed of narrow streets and an endless number of small shops, among which the slightest traces of the Jewish quarter on Carrer Marlet can be glimpsed, like the indestructible imperial walls to which a wealthy medieval residence in Pati Limona clings, or which simply surface in the nameless little Plaça dels Traginers. Once past the perfect borders of the Gothic Barrio and the "wound" of the monumental Laietana Road, opened between 1908 and 1917 to bring oxygen to the asphyxiated roadways of the old city, the streets resume their normal size, undoubtedly inadequate for appreciating the creative delirium presented by the Palau de la Musica Catalana. The masterpiece of Lluis Domenech I Montaner looks onto the narrow street of S. Pere mes alt at the beginning of the neighborhood that has taken its name from the old abbey. Inaugurated in 1908 as the headquarters of the Orfeo Català, a chorus founded in 1891, the building was transformed into a symbol of the rebirth of the Catalan artistic tradition and of Modernism itself, conceived by its designer as an "overwhelming voyage through music." If its façade in red brick, embellished with mosaics, columns, and a powerful sculptural group, does not entirely impress, the great hall of the auditorium, with its glass walls and thousands of natural reflections that rain down from its dome, is a unique work of art, enjoyable beyond its excessive decoration.

51 top left A big, upside-down dome-shaped skylight floods the concert hall of the Palau de la Musica with multicolored light.

51 top right The spectacular gallery surrounding the hall of the Palau is decorated with precious columns covered with mosaics and chandeliers.

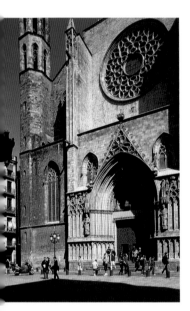

The street continues as far as the triangular square occupied by the remains of the abbey of St. Pere de les Puelles.

The ancient Latin-named monastery was incorporated by the city into its second circle of walls, together with the populous neighborhood that grew up around it.

Its foundation predates the year 1000, but its present-day appearance has been greatly compromised by the passing of the revolutionary craze and by a poor restoration during the last century from which a few Romanesque remnants inside and its lovely fifteenth-century portal were spared.

All around, in the crowded streets with a more diverse population, Gothic palaces and old graffiti, alleyways, and courtyards from the recent industrial-era past are found under siege by radical renovations, which in a few months can change the face and cultural identity of the neighborhood.

Nothing in Barcelona is more changeable than squares and streets in the old city. Carrer de la Princesa, the other legacy of the Roman road layout, separates the Barrio of St. Pere from the Ribera, the ancient sailors' quarter, once teeming with porters devoted to the Virgin Mary of the sea. In line with many other parts of Barcelona, La Ribera is rapidly changing but not always in its entirety relative to its centuries-old traditions.

Therefore, it is no use looking for old markets that until a few years ago kept businesses alive that had been handed down for generations: the dogmas of the modern economy do not allow for sentimental commerce. A few spots still manage to maintain a special charm, tied to the intense existence that over the centuries has characterized the neighborhood. The skeleton of the old Born Market deserves more than a quick glance, whereas the Passeig of the same name heralds the solemn Gothic church of St. Maria del Mar, called, for its size and beauty, "the cathedral of the Ribera." A true masterpiece of the faith, it was erected as planned by Berenguer de Montagut within a few years, between 1329 and 1384, according to his design of absolute stylistic purity. On the façade opens a single portal from which emerge the statues of Saints Peter and Paul and a big rose window inspired by the original destroyed in a fire in 1428.

However, the interior is what is really surprising with its unusual perspective due to the large distances between the columns, which make it look more like "an immense hall rather than the gallery typical of other Gothic churches," observed the writer Alexandre Cirici. No superfluous element distracts from prayer, whereas one's gaze can freely range beyond the gorgeous stained-glass windows covering its walls. Outside, on the right side, at the site of the church's ancient cemetery, a space was completely redesigned in 1986 to honor the fallen heroic defenders of the siege of Barcelona in 1714 that are buried there.

53 top right The old market of the Born, opened in 1876, closed its doors in 1971 and still awaits the total restoration project that will alter its purpose.

Some jasmine trees planted in the square recall the name given the burial place: Fossar de les Moreres. In the fourteenth century, the city's aristocracy also clustered near the big religious center, erecting their palaces on the street that took its name from an important medieval family that distinguished itself in the conquest of Maiorca: the Montcada family.

For centuries, the street maintained its noble status and still today preserves a patrician feel, containing a series of important cultural institutions. Every stone of its palaces is the custodian of works of art belonging to museums or private galleries.

Thus, the palace of the Marquises of Lliò holds, behind its fourteenth-century façade, the Museum of the Textile Arts and Costumes, the Dalmases Palace, with its gorgeous courtyard, a "baroque space" run by the Omnium Cultural Association, and the sixteenth-century Cervellò Palace, the famous Maeght Foundation and Art Gallery. However, the greatest attraction on Carrer Montcada is the Picasso Museum, probably the most popular in the city.

The gallery occupies five old buildings, added over the years to the original site located on the Berenguer d'Aguilar Palace.

The museum, put together thanks to various donations – beginning with the collection of Jaume Sabartes, followed by that of his personal secretary and finally by that of Picasso himself – documents the entire, extraordinary life of the artist. The museum is also especially important for pieces from the artist's youth, among them those of the famed "blue period," without forgetting the entire room dedicated to the "Meninas," a tribute to the great Velazquez. Looking back in time, remembering the Francoist Regime is amusing, which, openly hostile to the great painter, insisted that the museum be called by the name of the building.

Proceeding along this route, envisioned as a hypothetical spiral, we again cross the Laietana Road to step foot in another quadrant of the old city: the Barrio de la Mercé.

Once again, the neighborhood identifies itself with its most venerated church, the Mercé, or Our Lady of Grace, built just after the halfway mark of the eighteenth century right in the middle of the Era of Enlightenment. Unlike the surrounding neighborhoods, the area has maintained its eighteenth- to nineteenth-century appearance, a period in which it developed rapidly and became a fashionable quarter. The church has a strange annex on its left side, where the portal facing onto Carrer Ample is a sixteenth-century insertion from the Gothic church of St. Miguel. This charming background, towered over by the dome bearing the image of the Virgin Mary, presents itself to those arriving from Carrer da Carabassa like an image out of the past marked by the crumbling aristocracy of its palaces, joined by two simple arches. "Minor" touches are offered up pretty much all around, such as in the Carrer d'Avinyò with the building called El Borsì, or in Plaça Escudellers, occupied by the giant surrealist sculpture by Leandre Cristofol. A bit more somber, the addition of Placeta Milans with its polygonal liveliness has revitalized a series of humble condominiums, whereas in an intact late-nineteenth-century setting, the Passatge del Credit, a simple plaque at number four commemorates the birth of the great painter Joan Miró. Still in the 1800s, under the arches of Plaça Reial, what may be the least Catalan of Barcelona's squares appears, a design by Francesc Daniel Molina dating back to 1848 and laid over the site of the ancient convent of the Capuchins. The square features one of the earliest whims of Antoni Gaudi, who designed the two multicolored street lamps at the sides of a central fountain; above all, the square has a series of historic café's that make it one of the liveliest and best-loved squares in the city.

After a few steps and a deep breath we are on the famous Rambla. "The Rambla is not an urban artery, it is a public vein that ends by injecting the city into the most venial part of your body, that is, the eyes," wrote Quim Soler in *24 Escriptors, 24 Hores a la Rambla*.

It is the place where the slow running of water towards the sea is replaced by the unstoppable flow of a human current. It is a human-sized avenue designed for the necessary simple pleasure of meeting and getting to know others. The Rambla is actually a plural entity, observing the old names that mark its sections. Starting at the Rambla de Canaletes, which owes its name to a fountain, one moves on to dels Estudis and then, continuing towards the sea, to Sant Josep, dels Caputxins and, finally, Santa Monica. Today, as in the big medieval fairs, one takes a walk to astound and be astounded, among the flowers and birds of unexpected colors and immobile street artists in this perpetually slow-moving tunnel. It is possible to daringly state that the Rambla was born out of the Counter Reformation, which filled an area previously empty and overlooked the border between the old, residential city and an indistinct countryside with convents and religious buildings. The eighteenth century again moved the city's center of gravity and, with the rapid industrialization of the Raval, the Rambla took its present-day position as an important road axis perpendicular to

the sea. Its appearance slowly took shape, assuming the upper-class tone of big European metropolises. Its transformation into a tree-lined avenue happened in 1859, a few years after the dismantling of the walls, and its shops soon became a tradition immortalized by the painters of the Sala Parés. In an attempt to make a summary description of its sights, we start from the top, where the increased slope favors a better perspective of the avenue. The Rambla de Canaletes distinguishes itself with its brevity and the fountain that gave it its name. Once famous for being fed by the waters of Montcada, the fountain gathered particular popularity to the point of being considered an authentic good-luck charm for local soccer teams. The pedestrian part regularly comes to life with stalls selling animals. Perhaps an anachronistic attraction, it transforms the Rambla dels Estudis into a piece of impromptu exoticism. Among its buildings, the sophisticated eclecticism of the Science Academy can be noticed, built by Josep Domenech i Estapà in 1883, which is also where the Poliorama Theater was also opened in 1912, in contrast with the austere simplicity of the eighteenth-century Moja Palace. A few feet ahead, we find the flashy side of the church of Betlem, a baroque building built by the Jesuits between the end of the seventeenth century and the beginning of the eighteenth century, whose opulent façade is almost absorbed by Carrer del Carme.

58 *Casa Figueras, on the Rambla, the work of Antoni Ros i Guell in 1902, is literally the most beautiful example of Modernism in the city.*

59 *The market of St. Josep de la Boqueria, built in 1840 over the ruins of the Carmelite convent, is today a triumph of colors and flavors that, despite its undeniable attraction for tourists, has maintained its original purpose as the main source for provisions in the old city.*

The intersection with Carrer de la Portaferrissa marks the part on the Rambla de Sant Josep where, having lost the perspective slope of the first tract, the "river" narrows into a gorge of flower-lined walls.

It is the richest branch, more attentive to esthetics and with brighter colors, which adorn both the houses and the stalls. Almost next to the building of La Virreina (1772-1778), which houses a cultural institute, is the most charming market in the city, Sant Josep de la Boqueria, an institution that originated in 1840 upon the ruins of the Carmelite convent, which burned down in 1835. To consider the market merely a tourist attraction would be a grave error because it is still the old city's main market, which willingly forgives the narrow vision of the passing customer.

As the flowers occupy the center of the street with their saturated colors, the walls of some of the houses seem to form the natural backdrop to this spectacle. We are speaking of the narrow "house with the graffiti" and, at number 83, of the most beautiful displays of Modernism on the Rambla: the old Casa Figueras.

60 top left The palace of the Rambla, which opened in 1992, makes it possible, with its innovative façade, to frame the old bell-tower of St. Maria del Pi from a new perspective, finally making it visible from the tree-lined avenue.

In sharp contrast with the dominant "floral" element, there is the so-called new palace of the Rambla, a big commercial building inaugurated in 1992, which like many other additions of modern Barcelona, attempts to make a personal insertion in the old city layout.

In this case, the winning element is the large opening on the façade that frames the octagonal bell-tower of Santa Maria del Pi, at first hidden from view.

This church is another wonderful example of Gothic style, given its present-day form between the fourteenth and fifteenth centuries. The interior has a single nave with two aisles, austere and basic, whereas the façade flaunts one of the biggest rose windows in the world, unfortunately destroyed during the civil war and later rebuilt. In the square before it, with its famous pine tree, the oldest graffiti in the city is the legacy of the house of one of its many guilds that contrasts with the solemn religious building.

Returning to the Rambla, the sight of the Quadros House greets us, the umpteenth example of Barcelona's endless architectural originality. The Eastern elements were designed by Josep Vilaseca in 1885, pre-dating by several years the more innovative and calculated Modernist tastes.

60 top right Placa del Pi (the pine tree): the city's oldest graffiti (1685) decorates what was the headquarters of one of the many gremios in Barcelona, the ancient guilds that formed the social and productive fabric of the city for centuries.

60-61 This detail is part of the frieze adorning the façade of the Quadros House at number 80 of the Rambla. An icon that preceded Modernist trends, it was the result of the restoration of an earlier building built by Josep Vilaseca in 1885.

61 top A Chinese dragon stands out from a corner of Quadros House, the exotic and fanciful expression of a fashion widespread between the nineteenth and twentieth centuries.

Officially, we are in Pla de l'Os, or Pla de la Bouqueria, but in reality it is only a widening in the roads, a crossroads where the Rambla dels Caputxins begins.

The mosaic by Mirò, placed in the middle of the square in 1976, symbolizes the artist's wish to bring his art to the squares and streets of the city, a tendency that would spread in popularity during the 1990s. Encountering the theater of the Liceu, however, evokes some of the most tormented pages from Barcelona's history and not only for the fire that destroyed the building twice, but for the tragic attack of 1893. The theater was the symbol of Barcelona's upper class when Santiago Salvador threw two bombs onto the stage during the second act of William Tell.

The crater separated the two sides of society at the end of the century even more profoundly: one dedicated to the pleasure of Modernist creativity and one of the misery embraced by anarchist ideas.

Past the arches heralding Plaça Reial begins the section dedicated to portrait artists who took possession of the avenue, substituting their easels for those bearing the menus of bars and restaurants. For a backdrop, their work has the first theater of Barcelona, long ago named Santa Croce, the first performance given in 1597.

The present-day, curved façade stamps a special personality on the building, known today as the Principal Theater. Seated in front of it since 1906, Frederic Soler Pitarra, the famous writer of popular comedic plays, watches everyone from his unquestionably bulky pedestal.

Like a river that loses its strength as it approaches the sea, the La Rambla, in its last tract called Santa Monica, widens almost to form a delta encompassing the last buildings.

On one side is the modern Centre d'Art Santa Monica and the ancient royal wharves and on the other, the Wax Museum and the so-called building of the Cannon Foundry.

The ideal "mouth" for this human stream, overlooked by the famous statue of Columbus, bears the name of Portal de la Pau, the "portal of peace," a space conceived in 1850 and thereafter enlarged to give the city closer contact with the Mediterranean.

64-65 *The Museum
of Contemporary Art,
in addition to its
permanent collection,
organizes numerous
cultural initiatives
and temporary
exhibits documenting
the careers of the great
artists of our time.*

64 bottom *The big
and luminous hall on
the ground floor of the
MACBA is perfectly
suited to be a
classroom favorable to
a playful approach to
art.*

Beyond the Rambla is the Raval, a tale that still awaits its ending. From an ancient flowering of convents, the area was quickly transformed into an industrial inferno, where within a few years, factories and smokestacks creating Dantean bolgias that imprisoned up to 40,000 men per square mile replaced places of meditation. This was the Raval. Its brief history of just three centuries was lived with incredible intensity, often ignoring the limits of human dignity and giving the neighborhood the deserved nickname of "Barrio Chino," given to it by journalist Angel Marsà. Then, there was its resurrection, to the point that it became a symbol for the great social and urban laboratory that is Barcelona. A strange phenomenon brings new cultural institutions to its poorest immigrants, recycles the old dives of the fictional inspector Pepe Carvalho into fancy restaurants and displays the remnants of its arduous past with pride. No risk of the boredom of habit is run by those who decide to cross the Raval, where the feeling of being part of an ambitious experiment is strong, despite being in touch with a difficult present. Traveling the lovely Carrer d'Elisabets, for example, one can sense the area's charm, even just by glancing under the porticoes of Plaça del Bonsuccés or into the church of God's Mercy, now converted into a modern bookshop.

A last look at the street falls on the Convent of the Angels and just outside the square one is inevitably struck by the flash of pure white light lit in 1995 by Richard Meier: Barcelona's Museum of Contemporary Art (MACBA). The museum is a challenge of enormous proportions acting as a catalytic center for a cultural movement in constant expansion.

This temple of art opens its doors onto a large pronaos made up of staircases and bare columns that gives way to white rooms, sacred to the difficult polytheistic cult of the cutting edge. Its lines are of an absolute conceptual purity, the ideal container for an enigmatic art composed of performances and exhibits that also welcomes the more famous schools of the second half of the twentieth century.

Behind the museum stands another prestigious institution, the Center of Contemporary Culture of Barcelona (CCCB), which took over a portion of the old Charity House.

The entrance to the Patio de les Dones, or "the women's courtyard," leaves no doubt about the breadth of the center's alterations of the space and the quality of the results. A bare and projecting façade designed by Helio Pinòn and Albert Viaplana makes the

most of the big exposition spaces and pleasantly encloses the elegant nineteenth-century square decorated with both inscriptions of a moral nature and with geometric and floral patterns.

Older and more compact is the Patio Manning, adjacent to the former, enlivened by lovely eighteenth-century majolica decorations and belonging to the ex-Charity House. On the wave of this "cultural tempest," the transformation is spreading to every corner of the Raval, which is witnessing the daily alteration of the relationship between spaces and old institutions in deterioration.

65 top   The old Convent of the Angels, found in Raval, was described as "The Garden of Convents," where today performances and contemporary-art exhibits are held.

65 bottom   The New Center of Contemporary Culture (CCCB) in Barcelona is located in the building where the House of Charity had its headquarters.

66 top The hospital of the Holy Cross dates back to the seventeenth century. In the rooms of the old complex, which maintained its original function until 1926, the National Library of Catalonia, among other institutions, has established its main branch.

66 bottom Plaça de les Caramelles, dominated by the rear façade of the sixteenth-century Convent dels Angels, was the result of rational and creative remodeling, based on the concept of a living space being necessary to the neighborhood.

66-67 The Cat by Fernando Botero is a recent acquisition for the Rambla del Raval, the big square that originated in 1995 in the heart of the neighborhood, after its extensive remodeling.

67 top left The hundred-year-old ballroom of the Palm represents one of the few remaining symbols of a vanished social class, whose focus on the pleasures of life, disseminated by Modernism, clashed with the hellish existence of workers in the nearby factories of the Raval.

umphal furnishings of La Paloma, a ballroom featuring an intact 1904 design and atmosphere. Likewise, little Plaça del Pedrò, so dear to the great writer Manuel Vàzquez Montalbàn, appears intact in its sad state. These are places where, as the writer himself said, "the Olympic pigeon" has yet to arrive. On the other hand, a place aggressively demolished is the area surrounding nearby Rambla del Raval, whose shape recalls a stadium from Ancient Greece. These were necessary interventions to restore long-lost dignity to the area, hailed by some for the unquestionably innovative stimulus they provided as much as they were protested by others for the weighty shadow of property speculation that hung over them. From one corner of the Rambla one can take Carrer Sant Pau, which leads directly to the church of the same name, perhaps the most important Romanesque monument in Barcelona. The small, Greek-cross-shaped building was rebuilt in the twelfth century overtop a building from the tenth century and features a simple yet noble façade from which emerge the figures of Christ between Saints Peter and Paul, the symbols of the four evangelists, and two Visigoth columns. Even more charming is the tiny fourteenth-century cloister enriched by trilobite arches: a medieval oasis that has survived intact and is still fulfilling its original function. Around the church, on other hand, the situation has undergone profound changes; and today, only a smokestack next to a large park designed in the 1990s recalls the Raval's industrial past.

This is the situation at the old Ospedale of the Holy Cross, which, surrounding the orange trees in its cloister, hosts the Library of Catalonia, among other things, or the happy and creative salvaging of Plaça de les Caramelles, which gave its inhabitants some basic space, unimaginable until a few years ago, and the real possibility of acquaintances running into each other. Next to these great works, however, surprises are not lacking. Hard-to-find spots hide little secrets, unintentional monuments to past tastes or to pure chance. In Carrer del Tigre, no Modernist touches displayed on the outside betray the tri-

67 top right "The romantic surprise" of St. Pau del Camp, in the area of the Rondas, is the most important period monument in the entire city. The modern-day building is a little church with a Greek-cross layout, rebuilt in the twelfth century on the same spot of the previous church. Remains of the fortifications and a delightful, thirteenth-century cloister are part of the complex.

68 For the chimneys on the roof of Guell Palace, Gaudi used the trencadis mosai technique, which became one of his most famous strong suits. It was based on the principle that waste does not exist in nature and that everything has a purpose and usefulness, thus transforming discarded ceramics into a precious and sophisticated material.

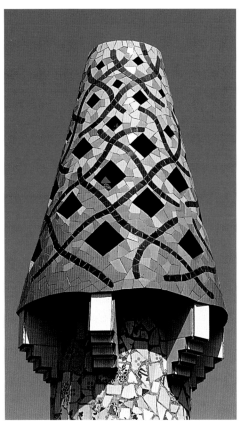

69 Other details explain the uniqueness of Guell Palace well. Whereas in the design of the façade and interiors, young Gaudi was particularly inspired by the neo-Gothic themes in fashion at the time, he fully expressed his creativity in the building's roof, giving rise to a veritable garden of colorful and fanciful shapes, seemingly lacking in any ties to tradition.

Lastly, the Guell Palace, which presents the large figure of its designer, Antoni Gaudi, and the complex relationship he had with this family.

It was an immature work, conceived between 1886 and 1890, which despite not having the sinuous and attractive lines of works from his later career, already demonstrate the great inspirational themes of his art: nature, Gothic style and faith. Some elements have an absolute originality, like the double carriage entrance, the columns in the cellar and the decoration of the reception hall.

However, the masterpiece of the palace, at least in some opinions, is without doubt the gorgeous assortment of chimneys on the roof around the conical dome. "Woods of the imagination," is an experiment in which Gaudi made use of a variety of materials, from marble to *trencadis*, meaning discarded pieces of ceramic.

A creative use of salvaged materials that would become a tell-tale symbol of his work, it was representative of the wholly Modernist belief in the functional renovation of art.

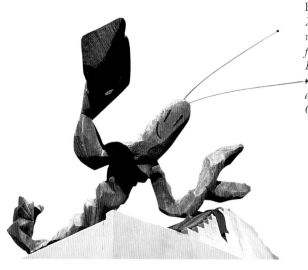

70 top The winking Big Shrimp by Xavier Mariscal waves to passers-by from the Moll de la Fusta, the old seashore returned to splendor during Barcelona's Olympic era.

70 bottom The futuristic structure of the World Trade Center contrasts with the traditional silhouette of the Montjuic telpher tower, in the city's old port.

70-71 The harbor is ringed by the old customs office, the monument to Christopher Columbus and the Moll de la Fusta, symbols of the seafaring, nineteenth-century and aristocratic Barcelona, respectively.

71 top left The Portal de la Pau (the Gateway of Peace), a balcony opening onto the sea and the "outlet" of the Rambla, is photographed here from the Colom Building.

71 top right The Passeig de Colom and the Moll de la Fusta have undergone radical transformations since the end of the 1980s, in order to adapt to city's new relationship with the sea.

Returning to the last part of the Rambla, or Ramblas, the statue of Columbus seems to indicate, from its 197-foot height, the direction to take to the sea – forever a great source of wealth, whose waves broke seemingly unnoticed on the shore until the Olympics when it was suddenly rediscovered and, in recent years, returned to being a main player in city life. The seaside delimiting the irregular boundaries of the old city has become another walkway of honor, a business card displaying its monuments and launching the perfect bridge to the future with the brand-new Rambla del Mar.

At the opposite end of the Moll de la Fusta, the long road's traditional name, the Rabmla del Mar opens onto the monumental Pla del Palau, in honor of the royal palace destroyed by fire in 1875. On one side, a heavy neoclassical façade completely hides the Gothic style of the Llotja, whose gem is the great hall, the work of Pere Llobet in 1387. As in many other cases, the square features historic build-ings of many highly different styles, eras and concepts. It is proof enough to mention the central fountain from 1856 dedicated to the "naked" Catalan Spirit and the four blocks of granite placed there in 1992 by the German sculptor Ullrich Ruckriem.

Opposite, almost forming a claw squeezing the sea, opens a historical appendix to the life of Barcelona, a neighborhood whose monuments are found in its people and everyday life: the Barceloneta. Its story was written in 1753 to offer dignified lodging to the evicted inhabitants of the Ribera by means of small, two-story houses, the memory of which has all but disappeared.

Then the factories came as well as the typical hard life at sea. The area is a slice of history in which workers and fishermen reigned supreme, a little Barcelona, with its crowded blocks clustered around the church of Sant Miquel.

Today, the Barceloneta looks like a strange but fashionable neighborhood threatened by rising property values, where there is a restaurant for every 120 inhabitants who still live in 300-square-foot apartments and had gone through the difficult period of the factory closures – "the sad Monday in the sun" of so many families. These stories can still be observed and imagined behind the elegant avenue named after Joan de Borbò and on the new beaches, fortunately more crowded on weekends.

72 top left Pla del Palau, developed starting in the early nineteenth century, owes its name to the original location of the royal palace, destroyed by fire in 1875.

72 top right The church of St. Miquel stands in Barceloneta Square. The building was started in 1753, the year in which the Marquis de la Mina founded the new neighborhood upon royal orders.

72-73 The inauguration of the recreational area of the Maremagnum (in the middle of the photo) has multiplied the number of seaside attractions,

stealing away from the monopoly held by the Barceloneta, with its long rows of golden houses, hundreds of little restaurants and popular beach.

73 top The so-called Palace of the Sea, an old, late-nineteenth-century warehouse, has held the Museum of the History of Catalonia since 1993.

73 bottom The Head of Barcelona, by Roy Lichtenstein, gives the gift of its smile to those who, from the seashore, want to direct themselves in the direction of the peninsula of the Barceloneta.

74 *The colossal urban renovation that brought the city closer to the sea, starting in the 1990s, led to the parallel development that saw the new beaches of the city as a valuable and absolutely necessary resource.*

75 *The Olympic Gift (1992) by Rebecca Horn is a tribute to the Barceloneta, the only true beach the city had before that time.*

76-77 *The lights come on at night. According to Montalban, Barcelona may have a thousand faces but remains a seaside city at heart, a place of passage, where the world comes and goes from its harbor.*

78 top Placa Catalunya is the undisputable center of the modern city and the main hub of metropolitan transportation systems. In the foreground is the monument to Francesc Macià by J.M. Subirachs from 1991.

78 center and 78-79 The Celebrity Murals is a unique work stretching across 4,800 square feet that portrays 26 personalities tied to the city's history.

78 bottom The bell-tower of Gracia is the symbol of the small town that was incorporated into Barcelona at the end of the nineteenth century.

79 top This Modernist-style building faces onto Placa Catalunya, whose urbanization was completed in 1927.

The nineteenth-century enlargement of the city, or the Eixample, is the crowning of the upper-class dream to live in a new reality, a utopia signed by the great artists of Modernism, first among them Antoni Gaudi.

It is indisputable that modern Barcelona is tied to the name of Idlefons Cerdà, whose urban planning freed the city from the medieval dimensions in which it lived, despite vast industrial development.

In 1859, Cerdà proposed an enormous enlargement that stretched from Montjuic to the Besos River, following a right-angled path formed by streets running parallel and perpendicular to the coast. It thus composed a homogenous pattern of big square blocks with rounded corners, or *manzanas*, 371 feet long per side, interrupted only by five wider streets: two large perpendicular roads, the Gran Via and the Passeig de Sant Joan, and three diagonal ones, two oriented along the imaginary lines of the earth (the Parallel and the Meridiana), and the third that crosses the web of the blocks diagonally (Avenida Diagonal).

The plan projected to build on only two sides of the *manzanas*, with no buildings over five floors high, to ensure all the apartments good light, whereas the rest of the area had to be devoted to public space, which, added to the new, tree-line avenues, would have created an ideal garden-city.

80 top Amatler House, by J. Puig i Cadafalch, along with Lleò Morera House and Batllò House, is one of the three elements in the so-called manzana de la discordia, *the most famous block on Passeig de Gracia.*

Widespread distribution of facilities, such as new schools, markets and civic centers demonstrates that Cerdà's conception saw the city as a social organism and not only as an architectural space.

However, the political discussion between the local authorities and the government arising over the plan's approval condemned it from the start to be mutilated in its entirety. Thereafter, the interests of landowners and property developers definitively distorted the project, stripping it of its ideological contents in favor of an elegant, upper-class urbanization committed only to showing off their own wealth.

The garden-city slowly transformed into a forest of houses with precious ceramic flowers and curved, wrought-iron balconies, leaving the real trees only along the long, traffic-ridden avenues. The history of the *Eixample* began at connection points with the old city, like Plaça de Catalonia, the center of modern-day life. An endless train of problems delayed its modernization, with a not entirely thrilling outcome. "The square has a surface area of almost 12 acres, a bit less than San Pietro or Place d'Etoile, but the comparison stops there," wrote the writer and journalist Josep M. Huertas Claveria, and not without irony.

A different success story was had by the triumphal Passeig da Gracia, opened prior to the clearing of the walls and forerunning to the big boulevards of the Eixample. The ancient country road that led to the first hills of the interior, towards the village of Gracia, was already, in the mid-1800s, a place for entertainment, illuminated by gas lamps, and later transformed at the end of the century into the upper-class' mostly highly sought after town: the city's Modernist display window par excellence. It is no coincidence, therefore, that in one of the octagons facing onto the street, three additions by the greatest personalities of the era, three completely contrasting, gorgeous designs, had clustered here over the beginning of the twentieth century. Thus was born the Manzana de la Discordia, a "work" as unintentional as it was admired by Josep Puig i Cadafalch, Lluis Domenech i Montaner and Antoni Gaudi.

Casa Amatler was the first to be rebuilt in 1900 by the young Puig i Cadafalch, who carved into the façade the "triumph of the decorative arts," as Alexandre Cirici Pellicer wrote. Sculptures inside, mosaic and marble flooring and stuccoes, multicolored tiles and wrought iron on the outside seemingly release a pure-pleasure esthetic in order to satisfy the expectations of its cultured and dynamic customer.

However, besides the architect, Puig i Cadafalch was a complex historical figure, archaeologist and restorer, tied to the themes of nationalism and old Catalan art, which he propagated through the innovative language of his creations. They were works inspired by Barcelona's Gothic splendor in which he also accomplished important public assignments, participating in political life as an urban scholar and planner. Among the residences bearing his signature, we should mention Casa Macaya from 1901. On its white façade, this happy restoration features the original capitals by the ingenious Eusebi Arnau, the promoter of new fashions in his time, which were raised to a place of honor by classical art.

80 bottom Granell House, a building with an original Modernist façade, is the work of architect Jeroni Ferran Granell i Manresa, who designed it in 1903.

80-81 Batllò House and Amatler House, with their unmistakable profiles, are two of the most charming sights to be found along Passeig de Gracia.

81 top This capital is one of the friezes in Macaya House, designed by Eusebi Arnau, an exquisite Modernist tribute to a symbol of progress.

Even Casa Serra, another of Puig i Cadafalch's works, should be observed in a special way, not only for its Modernist alchemy, but above all for the 1987 enlargement using an impenetrable glass surface. Of a different size, Casa Terrades, from 1905, is better known as "Casa de le Punxes." It is one of the most famous Modernist buildings in the city, in which stylized medieval elements raise the house to the rank of castles, and whose big tile panels displayed on the façades recall the obsessive themes of freedom and Catalan independence. The Lleó Morera House, the second component in the discord, was done by Lluis Domenech i Montaner.

A house conceived as an overall work of art, its designer arrogated the role of director of a vast orchestra of artisans; it is a fully mature work, admirable for its arabesque forms, rounded balconies and its little tower envisioned to be like a small temple. However, it is the interior of the residence that above all represents one of the most opulent and best preserved examples from the period, in which the magnificent window of the dining room continues to reign supreme. Even Domenech i Montaner, architect, historian and politician was much more than just a builder. A cultured and passionate humanist, theater and music lover, student of botany and zoology, as well as talented at drawing, he was the full incarnation of what were the ideals of the "Renaixenca."

82 Can Serra, the work of J. Puig i Cadafalch in 1908, underwent a bold enlargement orchestrated by A. Milà and F. Correa.

83 top Terrades House, better known as Casa de les Punxes, is one of the most famous designs by J. Puig i Cadafalch, conceived stylistically and in terms of size as a veritable medieval castle.

83 bottom Lleò Morera House, by L. Domenech i Montaner, is crowned by a delightful little tower shaped like a small oriental tower.

84 and 84-85 The hospital of Sant Pau, the biggest Modernist complex in Europe, was started by L. Domenech i Montaner in 1905.

85 top These pavilions are part of the hospital of Sant Pau, built between 1905 and 1930. The hospital is a

monumental complex stretching across 32 acres and included on UNESCO's artistic heritage of humanity list.

In addition to the already mentioned Palau de la Musica and the Lleó Morera House, many other works bear his signature, among them the Sant Pau Hospital, which is without doubt the most important.

Considered the greatest European Modernist monument to the extent that it was included in UNESCO's artistic heritage list, the hospital covers an area of 32 acres, in which every corner is cared for down to the smallest detail, from the monumental entrance housing the administrative offices, to the specialized wings and even the laboratories and other facilities.

Its restoration was envisioned as a garden-city, on the French model in fashion at the time, and construction was conducted in two different periods,

between 1905 and 1930, the second period of which was managed by his son, Pere Domenech i Roura. Its magnificent design allowed for 48 pavilions positioned according to a rational urban plan, a citadel of pain enlivened by the cheerful forms and the joy of art, inspired by the modern concept of the psycho-physical combination of human nature. Within this vast production, the building of the present-day Tapies Foundation, from 1886, is also worth mentioning for it is considered the city's first example of Modernist architecture, in addition to some private homes, each of which is characterized by sophisticated esthetic choices, like Lamadrid House, Thomas House and the Montaner Building.

The third component in the discord, the Batllò House from 1904-06, is tied to the extraordinary figure of Antoni Gaudi. It is the architect's "civilian" masterpiece, the sublimation of a supernatural vision and, at the same time, a blend of the historical and esthetic ideals of the Modernist movement.

The building is a unique prototype of shapes and colors molded in soft and enveloping light found in every line of the structure. Even the elegant forms of the Amatler House become an ordinary archaic remnant next to the sinuous grills on the balconies and the undulating roof shaped like a mythological dragon.

Designed at the height of his maturity, at 52 years old, Batllò House is a work independent of Gaudi's favorite stylistic expressions, in which his Gothic, baroque and natural influences are abandoned to follow a creative impetus of universal value. Technically, it is only the restructuring of a building bought by the textile industrialist Josep Batllò to be his home, but the result of the construction exceeded his wildest imagination. Its pure beauty is a pleasure to behold on cold winter mornings, when the clean and radiant light warms the infinite tile raindrops on the façade and strikes the enamel shards on the roof.

Like the entire city, Battlò House is built in the rough stone of Montjuic, which on the main floor, however, takes on smoothed forms with a natural appearance, whereas the upper floors smile in a thousand colors from enamels, stained glass and lively balconies.

A dragon or the bottom of the sea, according to running interpretations, covers the roof, full of reflecting colors and molded shapes, from which rises a bulb-shaped cross. The seductive feel emanating from the inside rooms is a total surprise, a feeling amplified by the lack of furnishings making it possible to observe the ingenious technical details created by Gaudi.

Light and air compose the volumes in an unremitting play of imaginary forms. On the main floor, the hall stands out, whose design develops around the spiral of the ceiling that extends down the walls, smoothing every corner to create a soft molded tension, transmitted even to the windows and doors. It is the triumph of curves and a discreet sensuality that can be noted above all in the fireplace, a masterpiece envisioned as an intimate shelter in warm and enveloping tones.

Every detail in the house is the result of a rational as much as an elegant concept. As proof, it is enough to consider the sublime technique used in the internal courtyard to capture and transmit light to the lower floors, employing ceramic tiles in different shades and windows with bigger openings on the bottom floors.

Such a highly conceptualized space is a totally revolutionary idea to architecture, when Gaudi seemed to be archaic in his beliefs. Born in Reus in 1853, Gaudi grew up carefully observing natural phenomena and its organic "sculptures," like the shells of snails and the shapes of trees, and soon learned "a sense of exact and three-dimensional handiwork" from his family.

When he got his degree in architecture, in 1878, the school's president was unable to hide his spontaneous skepticism, predicting for the young pupil either a total failure or an outstanding career. His work has been interpreted in several different lights, but some lines of thought can be traced back to very precise periods.

In an early period, the strongest influences were those of eclecticism and the neo-Gothic, like the Guell Building, the Vicens House and the Theresian College, whereas a completely individual language developed thereafter, a livelier style, if you will, one closer to the canons of Modernism, like in Guell Park and the Pedrera, as well as the previously mentioned Batllò House.

On Passeig de Gracia, a few *manzanas* ahead, another artistic symbol of Barcelona is found, the Milà House, widely know as La Pedrera. This giant sculpture is the umpteenth confirmation of the genius of Gaudi, who was the first to design a structure lacking in bearing walls, replaced by a weave of pillars and metal beams to support the vaults.

The solution eliminated the load on the walls that, now reduced to simple dividers, could be placed as desired on the floor, adapting spaces to any need.

The architect from Reus had created the concept of open space, later spread by Le Corbusier.

However, the disagreement between Gaudi and Rosario Segimon i Artells, the wife of Pere Milà, born of esthetic but above all financial differences, caused the breaking of the contract in 1910.

This "sin" left the building incomplete, still lacking the sculptural groups called for in the original design, and suspended its extraordinary destiny until a few years ago. Fortunately, the latest restoration saved the original colors, returning dignity to the stone waves on the façade and the twisted, wrought-iron balconies, attributed to J.M. Jujol, in which it is possible to see the seduction of surrealism or the twisted wreck of a train crash, as said at the time by its critics. This large container of surprises could not be lacking a roof, with its marked theatricality.

91 top and center The Piso of the Pedrera is an apartment in the building furnished with period furniture, which illustrates the functionality and surprising modernity of methods thought up by Gaudi.

90 This view emphasizes the grace and radiance of a staircase at the entrance to the apartments of the Pedrera. The great attention paid to each detail is worth noting, beginning with the decorations on the ceiling and the original design of the wrought-iron railing.

Upheld by a row of parabolic arches that determine the change in slope and its effect, it looks like a "garden of warriors" with chimneys and ventilation towers in futuristic and anthropomorphic shapes. It is like walking suspended in the dream-world of Gaudi, a fantastic place that has inspired a vast body of literature in search of the most mysterious symbols. Countless details in the internal design attest to the contemporary nature of his ideas, but above all, "his dogged search for a perfect situation."

When he stopped working on Pedrera, the last period of Gaudi's artistic life began, by then wrapped in deep asceticism, hanging between an obsessive mystical vision of life and a disconcerting creative capacity.

91 bottom The ceilings of the Pedrera, supported by an endless series of parabolic arches, hang above what has become the location of the Espai Gaudi, a permanent exhibit displaying the construction techniques and designs of the great architect.

The Espiatory Temple in Sagrada Familia, which he had been building for years, became symbolic of all his works, his house and his own grave.

The origin of that last great cathedral is linked to the history and skyline of twentieth-century Barcelona, a phenomenon that deserves to be known and free of the ideological prejudices that have accompanied it. The initial design came from Francesc de Paula del Villar, as wanted by Josep Bocabella, a rich librarian that financed the construction in 1882 to give the city a big expiatory temple.

Gaudi, who stepped in the following year, developed a much more ambitious idea, in which he respected only the layout of the building as stipulated by contract according to a basilica-like plan.

The classical neo-Gothic style disappeared from the quick and incomprehensible sketches of Gaudi, who repeating the same steps several times, decided to reform the cathedral into a forest of stone, a temple of Mediterranean Gothic, free from the buttresses in northern architecture. The model for this large institution can be seen right in front of all of us: nature. Thus the giant columns in the nave bend and fork, like tree branches, to support the weight of the vaults without external help.

"The architect of the future will build by imitating nature, because it is more rational, longer-lasting and lim-

ited in methods," said Gaudi, as his imagination pursued a utopia-like perfection. Thus, while inside the seed of this forest sprouted, the outside transformed into a luxuriant sculptural garden that rose high into the air.

In fact, the construction developed in sections and not in horizontal layers, respecting a perfect pattern of symbols. In this way, Gaudi was able to have the first façade, the Nativity scene, rise almost all the way to the top, along with the construction of the crypt and the apse. His death dealt a hard blow to the giant construction site, which resumed work only many years after endless and exhausting debate.

94 *In this overall view, the harmonious simplicity of the sculptural group emblazoned on the façade of the Passion can be appreciated.*

94-95 *Sagrada Familia, the last of the great cathedrals, is still an enormous construction site, whose maintenance depends on donations from worshipers and the proceeds from visitors.*

The same abuse was also heaped upon Josep Maria Subirachs, the artist that, since 1987, has "dared" to carry on the sculptural work on the façade featuring the Passion of Christ, the second one, begun in 1955.

Besides these two, oriented east to west, a third is envisaged in the final design, that of the Heavenly Glory, which will filter the midday sun, whereas in the twelve towers, the tubular bells invented by Gaudi himself will be installed. The forest of columns, with their five naves, will support the central 558-foot-tall spire, which will be topped by a big cross and surrounded by another five towers in honor of the Virgin Mary and the four evangelists. Construction continues because there is no doubt that the modern world has a large number of sins to atone for, just as asked for by the building's founder. As one of his biographers wrote, "Gaudi seen without his faith would be incomprehensible. Non-believers can love aspects of his work but not the whole." We can only wonder if the humble genius would have approved of being famous in this way.

95 top The clusters in which the pinnacles of Sagrada Familia's spires end can be clearly seen in these details, which in their finished form will be crowned by a central tower 558 feet tall.

Once outside the place of worship, the "earthly" dimension of the Eixample resurfaces domineeringly, immersed in its monumental as much as suffocating reality. It is necessary to look with patience, enter into a few *passatges* or even into the courtyards within some blocks to discover traces of what Cerdà dreamed of and hoped to accomplish.

The search for greenery concludes quickly in a few, tiny gardens, often carved out of intersections or in the middle of some avenue. Escorxador Park is an exception, located at the bor-

achieved an old aspiration: to free itself of the Citadel, a symbol of the defeat and terror perpetrated after 1714.

Once the fortress was destroyed, between 1881 and 1884, a park was created according to designs by Josep Fontserè i Mestre, imitating the style of those in London and Paris, inspired by the concept of "gardens are to the city as lungs are to human beings." Today, in one of the few military buildings saved from destruction, the parliament of Catalonia has its headquarters, inaugurated in 1932, closed during the

96-97 The waterfall in Citadel Park, built according to designs by Josep Fonserè, was completed thanks to the contribution of several artists, among them the young Gaudi and V. Vallmitjana, the sculptor of the Chariot of Aurora, the sculptural group crowning the fountain.

97 left The Monument to the 1888 World's Fair, a modern work by A. Clavè, stands in Citadel Park.

97 right The building of the Catalan Parliament, in Citadel Park, is located in the old arsenal built in 1727. Used for the first time in 1932 as the chamber of representatives, it became the home of the museum of modern art during the Franco period, only to return to its present-day function in 1980.

der with the Sants neighborhood, which it dominates with its gigantic sculpture entitled *Donna and Bird* by J. Mirò. Still, surprises are not lacking in discovering the curious courtyard of the Tower of the Aigues or the delightful Passatge Permanyer, with its little, pastel-colored villas. Great efforts were made to reacquire lost spaces, from a square carved out of an ex-factory to the Sedeta and to small installations of street art, like the countless sculptures or the mural of the 26 celebrities, which cross their slightly confused gazes across the long diagonal. The Arch of Triumph and the Park of the Little Citadel, the legacy of the World Exposition in 1888, the first important exhibit event hosted by industrialized Barcelona, deserve a chapter apart. After the revolution of 1868, Barcelona

years of Francoism and reopened in 1980. However, dominating the park are the gorgeous green areas that revolve around the pond and onto which flows the famous waterfall. On the side facing the old city, on the other hand, there is the Castle of the Three Dragons, built as a restaurant for the exhibit of Lluis Domenech i Montaner. Considered one of the first Modernist constructions in the city, since 1920 it has contained the Museum of Zoology. Along the avenue, the large iron and glass greenhouses complete a charming and relaxing stroll, to be enjoyed even beyond the park, as far as the Arch of Triumph marking the exhibition space's entrance. It makes a lovely snapshot from the late-nineteenth century of a city anxious to show the world a new style, progress and its renewed wealth.

THE MONTJUIC:
THE CATALAN OLYMPUS

The mountain of the city's origins, respected and feared, honored its greatness in the twentieth century by hosting the monumental 1929 exhibition and, more recently in 1992, the twenty-fifth Olympic Games.

Montjuic, or the Mount of the Jews, is the location of the city's origins, a myth that got lost over time since the city chose the sea as its true calling. It is a special mountain, where the voices of life are heard in its arenas, where the most playful art of the twentieth century, that of Joan Miró, found its perfect abode, and where the dreams of glory of so many athletes were crowned. Historically, Montjuic was the stone quarry for the houses of Barcelona and the immense granary that furnished bread until 1915. It is a mild mountain, yet feared for the big star-shaped castle dominating it, a re-

minder of Bourbon torture and oppression. The castle offers the best point from which to observe the city, with a view hanging dizzyingly over the sea that grows softer further inland, cloaked in green and full of Mediterranean character. Beyond the moat of the fortress, the slope is covered by a tumble of gardens bearing the names of illustrious men and poets, spaces that speak the language of flowers alongside the most diverse artistic expressions. Classic monuments, like that at the Sardana, the national ballet, coexist with more abstract interpretations, like the works in the little Garden of the Sculptures, or with magnificent settings, such as the Esplanada Olimpica, one of the best-known symbols in all of contemporary European architecture. Beloved traditional sites are not lacking, such as Laribal Park, featuring its Font del Gat so fashionable in the late-nineteenth century, which with its countless terraces descends as far as the Greek Theater, the outpost of a large space the city recently devoted to public use by converting the old flower market into a permanent theater complex.

Furthermore, Montjuic inherited popular attractions left behind by the 1929 exposition, like the Magic Fountain, which in its present-day manifestation enchants summer nights with its fascinating show of water, colors and music, or the Poble Espanyol, a realistic reproduction of monumental Spanish architecture, used as a public handicraft center.

98 Montjuic Castle is an eighteenth-century structure that, in the past, has represented the symbol of Bourbon repression. The home of the military museum, as well as being a perfect spot from which to admire the harbor and the city from above, is about to be transformed into a museum of peace.

99 On the side looking onto the city, the mountain of Montjuic features a series of carefully tended gardens, which form a vast recreational area sheltered from urban pollution.

100 top The photo portrays a moment from a performance of "free theater." At the base of the mountain, a significantly sized cultural center has taken shape, composed of structures and spaces reserved for various expressions of world theater.

100 bottom and 100-101 Pueblo Español, a reconstruction of the famous places and monuments of Spain, was created for foreign visitors to the 1929 Expo.

101 top left Even an Andalusian alley was recreated in Pueblo Español, today transformed into a lively artisan village.

101 top right The small sculpture garden, located on the side of the Mirò Foundation, is a space decorated with works by young contemporary artists.

102 From the terrace of the National Palace, one of the most fascinating views of Barcelona can be enjoyed, encompassing the entire monumental axis of Plaça de España, getting lost among the neighborhoods in the city outskirts and extending as far as the Basilica of the Sacred Heart, which crowns the mountain of Tibidabo.

103 The magic fountain, with its endless combinations of sounds and lights, is one of the most popular attractions on a long summer Barcelona night.

Usually, one gets to Montjuic by way of Plaza de Spagna, passing under the Venetian Towers and the historical buildings of the Fair. The entire complex, formed of fountains, staircases and gardens leading up to the giant National Palace, has a single origin: the 1929 World's Fair, an event that Barcelona strongly wished to host again after the success of the 1888 exposition. Preparations began as early as 1917 but suffered delays because of political issues in addition to technical. Barcelona, nonetheless, was a city that was exceeding a million inhabitants, ambitious, and with a driving industry that had brought about the subway system, electric lights and cinematography.

The exposition meant, on one hand, the triumph of monumentalism, but on the other, the consecration of a more sober style (the Noucentismo, or twentieth-century-ism) and the first appearance of a new architectural style for Catalonia, with the amazing German pavilion of Mies Van der Rohe, the very essence of Bauhaus. It was a smaller-sized building with lines of an absolute purity without any ties to the superfluous Mannerist expressions of the other structures. Misunderstood at the time, it was torn down at the end of the exposition but fortunately rebuilt between 1985 and 1987, finally recognized as a masterpiece of modern architecture. The outline of the exposition was intended to follow a grandiose monumental axis that departed from the ring of the Plaza de España, adorned by a fountain by Josep M Jujiol and Miquel Bay, and continue along the Avenida Maria Cristina, passing under the Venetian Towers, the work of Ramon Raventos.

The avenue was built to be a walkway of water and light, with glass columns that lit up to create fanciful effects.

Flanked all along by the various pavilions, it features the well-preserved palaces of Alfonso XIII and his consort Victoria Eugenia designed by Josep Puig I Cadafalch, with the exquisite little towers inspired by the Royal Bridge of Valencia. Other important buildings remained at the edges, immersed in the greenery, like little Albeniz Palace, which contained the royal pavilion, restructured and decorated by Salvador Dali in 1970.

In the setting, however, the National Palace, the most impressive monumental expression of the era, dominates unchallenged with its Spanish-Renaissance style.

Since 1934, it has been the headquarters of the National Art Museum of Catalonia (MNAC), an institution that has collected masterworks of Romanesque and Gothic sacred art, enhanced by the essential architectural frame studied by Gae Aulenti.

Beyond Laribal Park, there is another prestigious museum, in the shimmering building that holds the Mirò Foundation, established and opened by the artist himself. Inaugurated in 1975, it has about 11,000 pieces, including paintings, sculptures and ceramics in addition to his almost entire ensemble of drawings, donated largely by the museum's founder, his widow and his close friend Joan Prats.

Joan Mirò was born in 1893 in the heart of the Gothic Barrio, to an upper-class family who forced him to attend business school along with that of the arts and to gain his earliest work experience as an accounting clerk. Very soon, however, young Mirò proved himself to be ill suited to work and, in 1912, determined to live off of painting. He enrolled in Francesc Gali's art school, which he attended for five years and where he met Joan Prats and Josep Llorens Artigas.

His initial contact with businessman Josep Dalmau and their first meeting in his gallery date back to 1916 and 1918, events that convinced Mirò to move to Paris. His pictures from this period openly reveal strong Cubist and futurist influences, though he continued to be interested in nature and realistic painting. Meanwhile, subjects already started to appear that, portrayed in endless versions, would frequently be repeated in his work: women, the moon and birds.

His first trip to the capital of art was in 1920, followed by his first personal show the following year, when he was already friends with André Masson, Jean Dubuffet and André Breton, among others. They were important years at the center of an intense avant-garde movement, but more detached from the high-society scene, in which the artist's personality matured while his relationships with Max Ernst and Hans Arp grew closer.

In 1924, the year of the *Surrealist's Manifesto*, Mirò was already creating dreamlike forms, unreal spaces that do not shy away from dream interpretation but rather from the contemplation of external phenomena that undergo an objective transformation. Stylized shapes and monochrome backgrounds represented ideas more than real facts, a parallel universe that put the picture itself in doubt. Between 1929 and 1930 Mirò celebrated his marriage and the birth of his only daughter and returned more often to Catalonia, where he spent, above all, summers, working at Montroig and in his childhood home in Barcelona. His first attempts at sculpture date back to 1931, whereas the following years mark his continued experimentation with the expressive power of collage.

108 top left The work of J. Mirò, the Great Carpet of the Foundation *is one of the Catalan painter's universally known masterpieces.*

108 top right The model for the sculptural group that stands in the heart of La Défense in Paris was done by Mirò in 1975.

108-109 The museum of the Mirò Foundation contains a total of about 11,000 works by the artist, among them almost the entire body of his drawings.

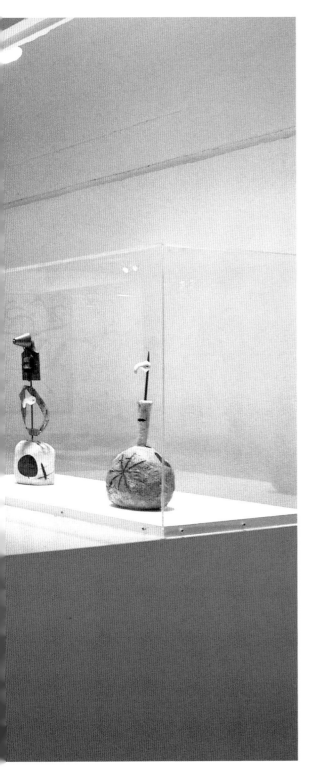

Mirò was an internationally famous artist that exhibited even in New York. When in the mid-1930s he noticed tension and fear due to the political situation in Spain, the colors of his paintings grew darker and the figures in his *Pinturas Salvajes* are often twisted and deformed.

He felt the coming of the civil war, from which he fled, returning to Paris until 1940 and then taking refuge in Normandy, following an uncontrollable desire to avoid and distance himself from the horrors of war.

In the post-war period, he was still busy experimenting with new techniques and materials, like ceramics and bronze sculpture, when in 1948, his association with Aimé Maeght was born, the Parisian businessman who wisely managed his work. In the 1950s, Mirò's fame reached its height, when he finished the large UNESCO murals in Paris and, within a few years, his first monumental-sized sculptures appeared.

His language is as open and flexible as the man is private and introverted. His cosmology, though perpetually evolving, always revolves around the same universal symbols that have appeared since the 1920s, man and woman, accompanied in their voyage by stars and planets.

In 1972, he officially founded the center for study that would bear his name and that he would open three years later. The last period of his life was dedicated to Barcelona, though he had long before retired to live in Palma di Maiorca, where his friend Sert had built him a marvelous villa where he could fully enjoy the Mediterranean light.

In 1976, he did the floor of Pla de l'Os, on the Rambla, whereas in 1982, he finished *Dona i ocell*, which would be erected in the new park of the Escorxador, thus fulfilling his wish to bring art to the streets and to make the city smile with the joy caused by colors and his disjointed characters.

From 1901, the year of his first preserved drawing, to 1983, the year of his death, his work had spanned the 1900s with the lightness typical of a child's dream, the inspiration for a universal language composed of shapes and pure colors suspended in a world that prefers fantasy to the laws of gravity. Mirò left the world right in the year in which efforts to promote Barcelona as a candidate to host the Olympic Games came together, the beginning of a giant challenge and the vindication of a failed attempt in 1936.

110 top left Utsuroshi (Change) is the name of the futuristic installation by Aiko Miyawachi, composed of cement and metal trees on the Olympic Esplanade.

110 top right The 1992 Olympic Games transformed the area of the Olympic Esplanade, using a clever combination of different styles and artwork.

The organization of the twenty-fifth Olympic Games, officially assigned to Barcelona on October 17, 1986, meant Montjuic's coming back to life, thereafter becoming a large area of urban development in the heart of the city. The plan created a monumental, vast space, starting with the remodeling of the old stadium, which a group of architects inserted into the middle of a magniloquent Olympic ring (the Esplanada Olimpica). The whole thing is formed by majestic terraces flanked by luminous columns, fountains and artistic installations, like the work by Aiko Miyawaki called *Cambio*, which serves as decoration for a new gem of contemporary architecture, the Palau St. Jordi.

Arata Isozaki's design is undoubtedly the most emblematic of Barcelona's revival, whereas the communications tower of Santiago Calatrava, with its 394 sculptured meters, is one of four elements that have changed the urban skyline of Olympic Barcelona.

In its shape, some have seen the legacy of Gaudi, well aware that the tilt of the shaft follows that of the earth's axis relative to the equator. In any case, it is a clear, not at all haphazard message of the "Olympic" will of those who wanted it built.

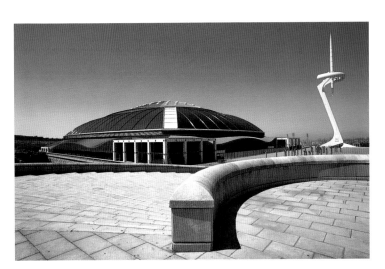

111

*113 top left A somber
façade characterizes
the Royal Palace of
Pedralbes, built
between 1925 and
1929 to accommodate
the sovereigns visiting
the World's Fair.*

*112 The cross of
Pedralbes, located just
beyond the walls of the
monastery of the same
name, is a modern
work imitating the
design of ancient
Gothic crosses.*

*112-113 In this view
from Montjuic, one
can see how the city,
towards the center,
has found its natural
borders only on the
slopes of the
mountain, after
having occupied all
the available space on
the plain.*

Gracia, Les Corts and Sarrià are the names of towns incorporated by Barcelona's expansion between 1897 and 1921. From small Catalan villages to city neighborhoods, often stripped of their essences, they hold more than a few hidden surprises and architectural gems of rare beauty.

From the beginning of the nineteenth century, the industrial and demographic growth of Barcelona expanded comparably to that of the towns surrounding it, which benefited the vitality of the city. During the century, in the circle formed by the towns of Sants, Gracia, Sant Andreu de Palomar and other municipalities, a large number of industries were founded that moved a healthy number of laborers to establish their residences there.

After the exposition of 1888, obsessed by its own growth, Barcelona planned the annexation of these villages, arousing inevitable local resistance and steady opposition from the government of Madrid. Capitalizing on the delicate political situation that was crossing the country, in 1897, the Barcelonese authorities saw the way clear for them to annex the towns on the outskirts, with the exception of Horta and Sarrià, which "capitulated" in 1904 and 1921. Finally, the great plan of the Eixample could be completed, even though it raised the need to link these urban nuclei to Barcelona.

A competition was announced in 1903 and won by the French urban planner Leon Jaussely, who, like Cerdà, developed a highly ambitious plan aimed at transforming Barcelona into the most beautiful city on the Mediterranean. Once again, however, the dream remained on paper, whereas in reality, a highly diluted version was adopted, approved only in 1917. This was a marginal problem though, if you will, when compared with the incessant need for lodging that motivated the venture. The one million inhabitants that within a few years had concentrated in the urban area required a quick fix more than any planned utopia, to the point that thousands of shacks sprouted up in numerous points around the city that were only partially able to be converted into public housing (the *casas baratas*). The situation did not, of course, improve during the period following the Second World War because of new waves of immigrants that created additional shantytowns lacking any hygienic conditions whatsoever.

In the 1970s especially, when the city was by now full, the housing problem spawned a disorganized and corrupt building policy, ending with the construction of an urban monster that one of its creators, the mayor Josep M. de Porcioles, euphemistically defined "big Barcelona." Worn down by endless siege and decades-long pressure, the old municipalities gradually lost their identity, preserving only the most prestigious monuments from the past, forced to coexist in the present with structures of a completely different value.

*113 top right
Pedralbes Monastery,
thanks to its stylistic
homogeneity, is a gem
of Catalan Gothic
art.*

114 Dos Rombs, *the work of artist Andreu Alfaro, is located at the far end of the New Diagonal in Cervantes Park.*

114-115 The Dragon, *the work of Basque sculptor Andres Nagel, was installed in 1987 opposite the new Sants train station.*

The first of these towns, west of the urban loop, is Sants, an old blue-collar village that maintained its industrial character until the 1970s, when it turned its factories over to a central role in city communications.

Just to the north, one enters the district of Les Corts, dominated by the sports complex of the Barcelona Football Club and where the Rodona Tower, an old house from 1600, holds an almost archaeological value in the context of the skyscrapers surrounding it, like an isolated frame from a lost film. Above the Diagonale, the upper neighborhoods of the city, in terms of income as well as geographical position, are found. Pedralbes, Sarrià and Sant Gervasi are the places were the last generation of well-to-do Barcelonese took refuge to escape the chronic lack of space and to legitimize their social status in the green of these last oases. Luxury residences blossomed around the ancient monastery of Pedralbes, founded by the legendary Queen Elisenda, widow of James II, in 1326. The monestary was consecrated only one year after its construction and is emblematic of the purest stylistic themes of Catalan Gothic, summarized in the harmonious cloister and simple, single-nave church.

Discreet urbanization, on the other hand, respected the perimeter of the Royal Palace of Pedralbes, built between 1925 and 1929 to house the sovereigns visiting Barcelona.

With its fleeting royal connection lost, it similarly maintains an impeccable dignity as the home of the Museums of Ceramics and Applied Arts, besides having a shady and relaxing garden.

115 top left Rodona Tower, an old seventeenth-century house, is the only are surviving from its time in this area now besieged by the skyscrapers of the New Diagonal.

115 top right Plaça de Sants, the heart of the old working-class neighborhood, has irreparably lost its identity since the 1970s, having become a strategic hub in the city transportation system.

A specific theme was also given to the Cervantes Park, the sweetest smelling in Barcelona, which features thousands of roses around the sculptures of Andreu Alfaro, in a remote corner of the city.

Around Sarrià, an independent municipality until 1921, the city maintains an elevated upper-class quality in its ancient, rural village layout, largely delegating the charm of the neighborhood to modernist attractions. Yet again, Antoni Gaudi is the main character in this itinerary, with works such as the Theresian College and the Tower of Bellesguard. The former of these buildings is a work of exemplary sobriety and elegance, executed with limited means between 1887 and 1888 and not lacking in ingenious solutions, beginning with the interiors. Though Gaudi had to contend with an already underway project, on the first floor he developed a new and complex composition based around a central courtyard that, with its zenith light, gave way to two parallel corridors of parabolic arches. This solution was able to create a mystical atmosphere, never gratuitous or for its own sake but rather as a means of prayer and for closeness to God. In 1900, Gaudi was also em-

ployed to build a private house on the spot where, in the fifteenth century, King Martin the Humane had placed his second home. The result this time was a castle, the product of a mature language highly evocative of the romantic story of the last Gothic king, in which the artist did not sacrifice his complete independence from the esthetic canons of Modernism. Too close to Barcelona to undergo any great industrialization but too small to reap any Olympic benefits, Gracia maintained certain privileges of a

small upper-class town inhabited by laborers and merchants, though it irreparably lost the charm of its little squares and lanes alongside the hill. Its countryside, the symbol of independence, is surrounded by a "new" anonymous phenomenon, as are the Plaça del Sol, the elegant Rambla de Prat and the Vicens house, one of the earliest visions of the ever-present Gaudi. An experiment in oriental-style shapes, it is covered in flowery majolica tiles in harsh contrast with the structure's dark bricks.

The floral theme of the wrought-iron fence, which reproduces palm fronds, would be faithfully repeated by Gaudi several years later in the designs for a garden-city that he worked on between 1900 and 1914: present-day Guell Park, the incomplete wish of his patron Eusebi Guell, who dreamt of a residential area surrounded by nature but near the city.

The main entrance to the park is flanked by two similar buildings, covered by ceramic shards and topped by a vigorous amanita and a double cross. They were the porter's office and a waiting room for visitors to the complex: a fanciful touch to the concrete bourgeois town.

Opposite the entrance is the staircase with the big famous *trencadis* lizard, a symbol of the town as well as of the park's, which leads to the room of the Doric columns with its slightly mysterious classical atmosphere, originally conceived as a community market.

118 top and 119 top Outcroppings, tunnels and stone walls interact playfully with the different levels of the hill in Guell Park, creating special and charming views.

118-119 The characteristic roofs of the buildings at the entrance to Guell Park reflect Gaudi's interest in the world of fables and were decorated using the characteristic trencadis technique.

119 right Gaudi worked on the design of the buildings in Guell Park for many years. In the top photo, one of the two houses at the park's entrance is shown, originally intended to be the groundskeepers' quarters.

The columns support a big terrace surrounded by twisted benches covered with designs made with ceramic shards in which various religious symbols can be noticed.

Once again, a mix of fantasy and spirituality always present in Gaudi's work, the symbolism hovering between the two is found in the coils of a long serpent in which lies a representation of the Mediterranean that then appears in its true form to those who then extend their gaze beyond the city. However, the surprises do not end here but rather hide in the rocky passageways formed by the buttresses created to overcome the rise of the hill in order to build the Museum House, where Gaudi himself lived until a few months before his death and which ends only at the top of the mountain, where the three crosses symbolic of the Trinity become one when looking towards the east.

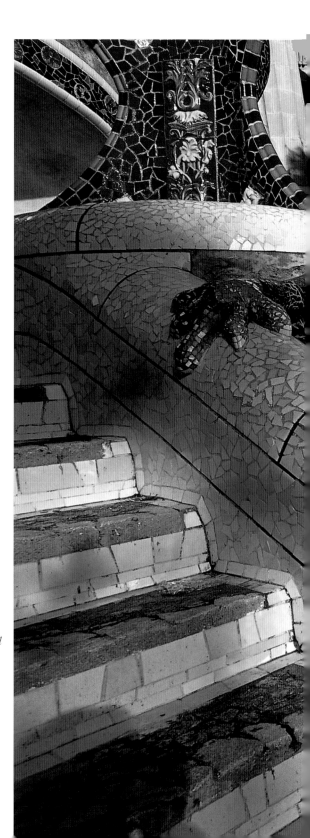

120 The famous and spectacular bench that surrounds the terrace of Guell Park is the work of Gaudi, completed with the help of the architect Jujol.

120-121 The well-known, big, trencadis-mosaic lizard, the symbol of Guell Park, was made, as were many of Gaudi's pieces, entirely out of discarded bits of ceramics.

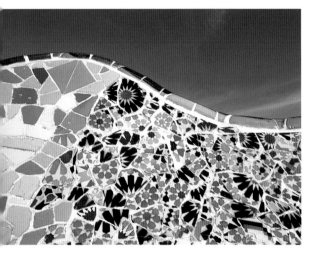

121 top left The entrance staircase to Guell Park is divided in half by a waterfall and ends at the top in the room known as "the room of the one hundred columns."

121 top right A soft wave of ceramic tiles enwraps the terrace of Guell Park. In the distance, the Gaudi House Museum can be glimpsed, where the artist lived before being layed to rest in the Sagrada Familia.

122-123 The Palace of the Ivies, a late-nineteenth-century work by the architect August Font i Carreras, was inspired by French castles and is surrounded by gorgeous gardens.

123 top A lovely neoclassical pavilion stands out at the top of a staircase at the end of the Labyrinth Park in Horta.

123 bottom In Horta, the famous Labyrinth Park stands in the middle of the park designed by the Italian architect Domenico Bagutti at the end of the 1700s.

Beyond the rise of Guell Park, the valleys and slopes of the old town of Horta are found, absorbed by Barcelona in 1904, when it covered a much larger territory that today bears the name of several different neighborhoods. Vall d'Hebron, which has preserved the name of the old monastery destroyed in 1835, is the most interesting, thanks to, or despite, the changes it has undergone.

Striking are the imposing Olympic structures, perfectly functional but perhaps oversized, like the giant steel sculptures completing the street furniture of the early 1990s, pleasant with their variety of colors and sturdiness of forms.

The most beautiful gardens of Barcelona, two gems recently acquired by the city but not terribly crowded, are found detached and protected from the traffic of the highways.

The Le Heures (The Ivies) Palace is a summer residence designed in 1895 by August Font i Carreras after a model of an old French castle, preceded by a terraced park, a veritable cascade of rose and lily perfumes, and shaded by palms and shiny magnolia trees. Next to this luxurious Golden-Era home, the municipality of Barcelona has presented its citizens with yet another product of an enlightened noble will: the famous Garden of the Labyrinth.

Designed at the end of the eighteenth century by the Italian architect Domenico Bagutti for the estate of the Marquis of Alfarras, the park combines the various fashion trends of the nineteenth century, emphasizing the structure of the already existing maze. This legacy is symbolized by a big sequoia, staircases and little temples climbing to a romantic pavilion and lush woods that hide the modern city from view.

At this point, the mountain of fun, the Tibidabo, the place where some-one said that "all of Barcelona can be seen without moving one's feet from the ground," deserves a glance.

Still a utopia, it is the creation of those who, in 1900, in the name of the Anonymous Company of Tibidabo, sought to transform the mountain into a city of gardens. An idea similar to that of Eusebi Guell, this case also proved unsuccessful and in the 1920s was converted into an amusement park.

However, its umbilical cord to the city, the Blue Tram and the centuries-old cable car that bring visitors to the present-day park and the temple of the Sacred Heart, has remained intact. At the top, those who dare to ride the Tower of the Waters, the "flying" at-tractions of the amusement park, or visit the panoramic belvedere of the church, can get a glimpse of the best view of the city, seduced by the latest colossal wonder of the Tower of Collserola. They all have an accom-plice: the beauty of Barcelona.

125 top right *The temple of the Sacred Heart of Jesus Christ on Tibidabo was erected in honor of the visit of Don Bosco in 1886. The upper portion of the structure, however, is more recent and was finished only after the Second World War.*

THE CITY
OF THE FUTURE

126 top This sculpture stands in the gardens of the Olympic Village, now a luxury residential neighborhood on the city's new, endless seashore.

126 bottom David and Goliath by Antony Llena (1993) is one of the works symbolic of the plethora of urban improvements that were planned for Barcelona on the occasion of the Olympic Games.

126-127 The city of the future adds to its vertical profile every day. In this photograph taken from Sagrada Familia, the new Agbar Tower can be seen, still under construction, and in the background, the skyscrapers of the new Diagonal Mar neighborhood.

Those who have had the fortune to see Barcelona several times in recent years, perhaps returning there after some time has passed, will have noticed that the city is radically changing.

Twenty years of frenetic work set off by the Olympic spark have moved the city's center of gravity and overturned the relationship between reality and its media stand-in. At first a seemingly crazy undertaking, it used the pretext of urban planning to free itself of the complex of being the "proud capital of a new homeland with old roots," which, however, suffers the present as "almost happy, painfully fertile," to use the words of Pere Quart describing the frustrating torment of Barcelona.

The city is suspended between its history as a great industrial metropolis and its current situation as an unfinished literary city.

In search of its image and a new personality, the city has torn out the old neighborhoods and opened itself up to the sea by widening the horizon and rediscovering its Mediterranean origins, which are mixing ever more with the colors of North Africa, Asia and Black Africa.

The desire surfaced to throw out lost decades, creating a more flexible economic model, modifying manufacturing and transportation strategies so that the city could adapt to the new urban expansion. A challenge in terms of image and content, the city has been thrown at the world and at itself, outspoken and fighting street by street, where art forms, traditional and non-traditional, mix with an everyday pragmatism in which the actors stand by either horrified or enthusiastic. The epicenter of this transformation can be found along the old rocky seaside, first blocked by industrial ghosts from the port and then magically transformed into miles of fine sandy beaches, which witnessed the birth of the Olympic Village at their back. *David and Goliath*, by Antoni Llena, is a work symbolic of this challenge, which commemorates the will to build the image of an open, tolerant city that cultivates a social vision defined by art and a taste for living well. This aspect is sought through an infinite number of exhibitions, as many as its galleries, museums and any other space suited to this purpose can accommodate. Love for Barcelona, the only expression tolerated by the Catalan pride during the Franco dictatorship, is the factor that made the survival of this city possible and that, with the advent of democracy, led it to its international consecration. The city of the future broke the old barriers by bringing the dilapidated Raval closer to the luxury of the upper-class neighborhoods and the strict lines of the Eixample closer to the villages of the industrial belt.

A widespread scheme of interventions was born, its brand clearly showing in the salvaging of areas marked by decline and in the creation of a new metropolitan design.

127 top left The point and beach of the Barceloneta, the "old" seaside of Barcelona, were photographed from St. Sebastian Tower.

127 top right In addition to having become one of the symbols of the city, the Olympic Towers, two twin skyscrapers over 492 feet tall, are the tallest buildings in Spain.

Joan Miró, a predecessor to this revolution, hinted at the period of reforms that returned living space and new views to the city in his monumental sculptures.

The old industrial zone of Sants, for example, stood in the spotlight in the early 1980s with the inauguration of its train station and the creation of an artificial landscape in the square in front. Conversion of the Espanya Industrial from a decrepit textile factory to a crucial "lung" for the neighborhood followed immediately thereafter.

Along with the new green space, a different relationship with artwork was also born, as suggested by the harmless dragon of Andres Nagel, which since then has willingly offered its jaws to playing children.

The rebuilding of the railway transportation system allowed for other important restorations, like in the Clot neighborhood, where an ambi-

tious archaeo-industrial design arose in the place of old garages, or at the North Station, equipped to be an Olympic site and then turned into a subtly charming park with its lovely sculptures by Beverly Pepper.

Fallen Sky, in particular, is a luminous tribute to the great artists of modernism that reveals innovative molded shapes and radiant color combinations. Sophisticated or sensational architectural concepts inspire masterpieces like the National Theater of Catalonia, Avenida Icaria or the amazing Agbar Tower, all conceived to achieve a goal much more ambitious than simple urban renovation.

Past this town, recreated from the constricted and rundown spaces of the old one, the colossal and protested project of Diagonal Mar, the last metropolitan frontier stepping from the natural border of the Besos River, has become reality.

128 The Tower of Catalonia, in the square in front of the Sants train station, frees itself with difficulty from the Dragon *by Andre Nagel, which seems to be swallowing it.*

129 top The park of Espanya Industrial, opened in 1985 in the Sants neighborhood, was created in the area once occupied by a big textile factory and represents a fundamental transformation in the urban landscape.

129 top center The Fallen Sky, *the work of Beverly Pepper, embellishes the park of the old North Station.*

129 bottom center At the base of the two Olympic towers, which stand guard over the new port, is the big Golden Fish

by the famous sculptor and architect Frank O. Gehry, a bronze sculpture over 160 feet long.

129 bottom The classical-inspired façade of the new National Theater of Catalonia is the work of architect Ricard Bofill.

130-131 Found in the park of the old North Station, the luminous and soothing pyramid entitled The Fallen Sky, by Beverly Pepper, originated as a tribute to the great artists of the past.

131 top left Terra i Foc by Joan Gardy Ardigas seeks in vain to compete with the imposing silhouettes of the skyscrapers of the New Diagonal.

131 top right The bridge of Bac de Roda, the work of Santiago Calatrava, is a structure that successfully blends functionality and esthetic values.

131 bottom The urbanization of Diagonal Mar originated out of a project planned completely for the future, in which even structures intended for recreational use were designed with the intention of defining a new trend.

Hosting the World Forum for Peace in 2004, Barcelona has again challenged itself, inaugurating impressive structures destined to alter the urban and social profile. At first glance, Barcelona seems a happy tireless city where there is a constant holiday atmosphere. A creative, night-loving, carefree city, it has mortgaged a secure future in order to devote itself to life's pleasures.

However, to more attentive eyes, the colossal effort that it is enduring to complete this last metamorphosis is noticeable. Barcelona's personal torment certainly could not escape the notice of Vazquez Montalban, the man who more than any other has contributed to making the city a literary one. With words full of sincere love, the writer describes the city as a woman searching for herself, a beautiful woman with a difficult personality in search of eternal love, "...the widowed and romantic capital of a lost empire,...captain of an industrial revolution,...sinner, dock worker, troubled....

Today, Barcelona, democratic and post-Olympic, has turned itself into a beautiful setting for a performance yet to be decided and is therefore predisposed to host any international event whatsoever, because there is no anguish more unsupportable than that of empty theaters.

Open to the sea, having befriended the sea, Barcelona has quit being the amphitheater of a hegemonic aristocracy to be one for an urban society conditioned by a strong patriotism for their beloved city, seen through the protective, enamored, Oedipus-like eyes of the children of widows, because the feeling of living in a city that never managed to marry well remains for the Barcelonese of today, like those of yesterday and tomorrow."

132 In this highly modern area, the World Forum for Peace and Friendship among Peoples was held, an occasion on which the city gave itself the gift of a new tourist harbor, among other things.

132-133 and 133 bottom This artificial landscape was created to integrate the futuristic buildings of the 2004 World Forum into its surroundings. It represents the latest challenge that Barcelona has made to itself and the world.

INDEX